Beat the Millennium Crash

Millennium Crash

How to Profit from the
Coming Financial Crisis

OTHER BOOKS
BY JAKE BERNSTEIN

Beat the
Millennium Crash

How to Profit from the
Coming Financial Crisis

JAKE BERNSTEIN

NEW YORK INSTITUTE OF FINANCE

NEW YORK • TORONTO • SYDNEY • TOKYO • SINGAPORE

Library of Congress Cataloging-in-Publication Data

Bernstein, Jacob
    Beat the millennium crash: how to profit from the coming financial crisis
/ Jake Bernstein.
        p. cm.
    ISBN 0-7352-0119-6 (pbk.)
    1. Stocks. 2. Speculation. 3. Investments. 4. Capital market.
5. Year 2000 date conversion (Computer systems). 6. Finance,
Personal. 7. Survival skills.   I. Title.
HG4661.B46 1999
332.024—dc21   99-22517
                                                    CIP

NYIF and NEW YORK INSTITUTE OF FINANCE are trademarks of Executive Tax
Reports, Inc. used under license by Prentice Hall Direct, Inc.

Printed in the United States of America

10 9 8 7 6 5 4 3 2 1

This publication is designed to provide accurate and authoritative information in
regard to the subject matter covered. It is sold with the understanding that the
publisher is not engaged in rendering legal, accounting, or other professional service. If legal advice or other expert assistance is required, the services of a competent professional person should be sought.

> *... From the Declaration of Principles jointly adopted by a*
> *Committee of the American Bar Association and a Committee*
> *of Publishers and Associations.*

ISBN 0-7352-0119-6

ATTENTION: CORPORATIONS AND SCHOOLS
Prentice Hall books are available at quantity discounts with bulk purchase for
educational, business, or sales promotional use. For information, please write
to: Prentice Hall Special Sales, 240 Frisch Court, Paramus, New Jersey 07652.
Please supply: title of book, ISBN, quantity, how the book will be used, date
needed.

 NEW YORK INSTITUTE OF FINANCE
An Imprint of Prentice Hall Press
Paramus, NJ 07652

On the World Wide Web at http://www.phdirect.com

CONTENTS

CHAPTER TWELVE
Panics, Pandemonium and Profits

CHAPTER THIRTEEN
Are You Ready?

PREFACE

What is my motivation for writing this book?

What qualifies me to express an opinion on this topic?

What are my goals?

These are all reasonable questions for which I hope I have valid answers. Perhaps my words and warnings will fall on blind eyes and deaf ears. I hope you will find some value in what I am about to tell you. Everything you will read in this book is based on history: the history of markets and economies, the history of human emotion and psychology and the history of societies.

My motivation in writing this book is to bring you to the edge of a vision in the hope that the vision illuminates a path. My qualifications are those of a man who has extensively studied, analyzed, written about, employed and scrutinized the intricate relationships among markets, economies, people, emotions, investor psychology, price cycles, governments and patterns of behavior.

My qualifications are not those of an academic. I was not educated as an economist, political scientist or mathematician. I was not schooled in history or anthropology. As the author of over 28 books on commodity and stock trading, investor psychology, cycles, seasonality and technical market analysis, I have some degree of expertise in this field. My education in clinical psychology and sociology has given me a unique perspective on markets, economics and human behavior. Inasmuch as all three are intricately intertwined, there can be no purely focused model of economics or market behavior without considering the effects of each aspect on the final result.

My goal is to inform you of what may, in my view, come to pass as the current millennium draws to an end and the new millennium begins. As you well know by now, opinions as to what may happen range from a passive long yawn by various blasé money managers to frenzied forecasts of Armageddon by bible-thumping fire-and-brimstone preachers. Some groups and individuals have sought to minimize the possible effects of a Year 2000 (Y2K) global computer crisis while others have capitalized on it, pandering to a panicked sector of the public. I consider each of these extremes unpalatable as well as foolhardy. Yet credible and reliable sources have expressed their concerns in no uncertain terms. Senator Robert Bennett, Year 2000 Tech Chairman of the U.S. Senate Hearings on Y2K, stated on June 12, 1998:

> I cannot be optimistic and I am genuinely concerned about the consequences of the millennial date change.

Before I tell you rationally what can be done about the potential problems, I'd like to tell you a little about myself, my view of markets, economies, financial institutions, governments and the individual investor. While my analysis may not be unique, I think you will find it concise, rational, far-reaching and specific. It is my hope that my suggestions will help you develop a program of personal preparedness that will serve you well in the event of a global Y2K crisis.

Despite my family and childhood history of adversity, I am an optimist. My parents were survivors of Auschwitz and Dachau. My early childhood was spent in poverty growing up in the mean streets of a Montreal, Canada slum. Extreme suffering can push a person to either of two extremes but rarely leaves a survivor unscathed. Having to worry and wonder if my parents would have enough money to feed and clothe my sister and me was the initial motivation for my achievements. Although I could easily have slipped into the culture of poverty, spending the rest of my life living on welfare and drifting without cause in a sea of minimum wage jobs, I did not. The horrors of my parents' experiences in concentration camps could have darkly colored my view of the world; instead, I was able to sublimate these feelings, and became a contrarian rather than an alarmist.

Although my formal education was in the field of clinical psychology, my fierce desire to avoid poverty and acquire wealth attracted me to the stock and commodity markets. I forced myself to study the essentials of economics and investing since I realized early on that these areas were truly the last frontiers of capitalism. They were the only areas where one could begin with relatively little money and accumulate sufficient capital to invest in other areas such as real estate and business. In pursuing my goals I admitted to the fact that my skills were severely limited. I devoured the writings of master investors and traders—gurus of Wall Street and LaSalle Street.

Initially, my quest for wealth was stymied by my inability to ask the right questions. In my naivete I failed to realize that my search for methods and tools was taking me in the wrong direction. While I struggled to find trading systems and techniques, I failed to grasp the substance because I was reaching for the shadow. Eventually I came to realize that the quality or process of my journey was more important than my techniques or my goals—that my goals would be attainable if my process was worthwhile, valid, and above all, self-fulfilling. With this recognition a whole new world of economic relationships opened its doors to my hungry mind and eyes. In the words of Ouspensky:

> ...All round me walls are crumbling ... horizons infinitely remote and incredibly beautiful stand revealed. It is as though threads, previously unknown and unsuspected, begin to reach out and bind things together ...*

I came to understand that all life and history, whether physical, economic, social or biological, could be viewed in terms of patterns. While patterns rarely repeat with exact timing, they are sufficiently repetitive to warrant study and continued monitoring. Only the dates and names of the players change; all else repeats. Given a broad perspective one can readily discern and extract patterns from one era to another, from one period of economics to another, and from one market environment to another. Undoubtedly, there are those who find fault with such a view inasmuch as it smacks of determinism.

---

* Ouspensky, P. D., *A New Model of the Universe: Principles of the Psychological Method in Its Application to Problems of Science, Religion, and Art.* New York: Dover Publications, 1997.

Yet nothing succeeds like success. In 1989, well before the economic madness of the 1990s, my book *The New Prosperity* provided a number of important long-range economic forecasts based on my understanding and analysis of economic patterns and cycles. Among my forecasts were the following:

- The collapse of the Japanese economy
- A persistent decline in U.S. interest rates until at least the mid-1990s
- Spread of the world economic crisis to communist countries
- Rejection of the prevailing view that the U.S. economy would enter a severe depression
- Major technological advances in genetic engineering and computer technology during the 1990s and beyond
- Major new developments in communications technology (now known as the Internet)
- New strength in the U.S. dollar relative to other world currencies
- The decline of Japanese business dominance and influence as their economy suffers a severe contraction
- Assertion that the direction of interest rates in the 1990s would be of paramount importance, and
- The most chilling forecast that a war was likely

But all of this was in the past. What does the future hold in store? While my cyclical views may have been essentially correct in the 1990s, what can we expect now as we embark upon the uncharted waters of the new millennium?

In analyzing and studying the historical market patterns in relation to the growing millennium madness, a number of thoughts occurred to me.

Viewed within the context of historical patterns, the Y2K hysteria appears to be nothing more than a replay of several previous periods of economic insanity and investor folly that swept the world on many occasions during the last few hundred years. While the Y2K problems we face are most assuredly real, the question *is not whether Y2K and its aftermath will present problems, but rather how we will deal with them.* I take for granted that there will be problems. It is what we do about these problems that will be of the utmost importance!

Many plans and programs are in place to minimize the possibly severe consequences that may accompany the arrival of the next millennium; however, the implementation of such "fixes" can be either facilitated or hindered by how we, as a people, act and react to the potential problems. My goals are to educate, illustrate and help you be prepared for what may come to pass.

I sincerely believe that although the problems we face may be severe and, in some cases, beyond repair, we have the national and global resources to overcome and/or avoid the serious consequences that may be unleashed by the so-called "millennium bug." Technology is only as strong or as effective as those who implement it. The true test of our progress in overcoming the problems that await us will be more a function of our emotions than a function of our technological preparation.

My more than 30 years in the markets have taught me that the weak link in the chain of any program, plan or system is most often the human element. While the world may be worried about the failure of computer systems come the Year 2000, *I am more concerned with the failure of human systems.* By this I mean that what concerns me most is not whether we will overcome the potential problems posed by the possible failure of computers worldwide to recognize the Year 2000 as a viable date but rather how people and nations react. We are being warned almost daily about the potential problems from supposedly informed sources. It is difficult to ignore statements such as the following from Senator Chris Dodd:

> You wouldn't want to be in an airplane, you wouldn't want to be in an elevator, and you wouldn't want to be in a hospital. . . . [C]ontingency plans . . . need to be put into place to minimize the harm from widespread failures.*

The best thing we can do is to prepare our investments and personal needs intelligently but not to excess. What's more, we need to prepare ourselves emotionally so that when and if crises do come, *we will avoid the panic that all too often exacerbates crises.* Success in all ventures such as these depends on preparation, organization, logic and a long view of history.

This book is as much about mass psychology as it is about strategic investments and the approaching millennium crisis. As I stated at the outset, I am essentially an optimist. I believe that we can overcome the

---

* U.S. Senate, Senator Christopher Dodd of Connecticut, Year 2000 Tech Committee Senate hearings on Y2K, June 12, 1998.

vast majority of potential problems that face us in the Year 2000 and beyond. But moreover, I believe that with the correct strategies we can even profit from the changes that await us.

This Book Was Written for You

This book was not written for professional market analysts or economists. It was written for the average investor, for the people, for the millions who strive daily to improve their lot in life and who are now threatened with a force so powerful and so unknown that they often feel helpless in its shadow. You may be confronted by numerous complex strategies for dealing with the problems of the new millennium. Ultimately I believe that investors will return to the basics.

Even though I will deal in this book with basic issues of financial survival and essential aspects of market patterns, professional money managers as well as business leaders and economists stand to learn a few new things. My view of economic patterns is not a traditional one. The relative simplicity of what I will tell you will not appeal to academia, yet such lack of appeal will not make my words any less true. This book will not bury you in a sea of technical terminology or the *lingua franca* of market analysis. Nor will it give you advice or expectations you can't understand without a degree in economics.

What This Book Can Do for You

- It will explain to you what the stock market has done, why it has done it, why things are about to change (if they haven't already by the time you read this) and what you need to do in order to prepare for the inevitable change in market direction as a possible consequence of Y2K.
- It will tell you clearly the signs and symptoms of an imminent change in direction. When you have learned them, watch for them and then take the necessary recommended actions.
- It will tell you what to do if and when these warning signs appear.

- It will give you a detailed plan of action as well as alternatives that you can use if the scenario unfolds differently from what you expected.

- It will tell you which market sectors are likely to suffer the most deterioration.

- It will tell you which market sectors are likely to remain strong or likely to resist the down turn in the event of a millennium crisis and market decline.

- It will give you insights as to how the coming millennium crash and market decline may affect your other investments.

- It will give you an idea of how and if the coming market decline and possible Y2K crisis will affect your bank or lending institution, and

- It will help guide you through the treacherous times that await all investors as the millennium comes to an end and as the new millennium begins (with a bang!).

What This Book Cannot Do for You

This book will not spoon-feed you. It will not give you a cookbook to success. It will not guarantee results, and it will not take you by the hand to make certain you take the necessary steps to protect your personal and business finances from the inevitable and unavoidable market correction (and its far-reaching consequences).

WHAT *NOT* TO EXPECT FROM THIS BOOK

- Do not expect me to recommend individual stocks to you. Rather, I will give recommendations in specific stock categories (i.e., precious metals, Internet, communications, automobiles, utilities, etc.).

- Do not expect me to be 100 percent accurate to the very date or week. My analyses are based on the lessons of history. Although I believe that history repeats itself, it does not always do so exactly. There are variations and individual differences each time. These differences must be considered within the framework of current events. I will provide the framework, but you will need to take some initiative as well, evaluating events within that framework.

■ Do not expect me to give you *all* the answers. The simple fact is that I don't know all the answers, but no one else does either. Investing and trading involve risk. The higher the safety, the lower the return on your investment. This is why Treasury bills and savings accounts pay very little and why high-risk investments can return a substantial yield.

Ultimately, you alone can make the decisions and take the actions that I recommend to you. Since you alone are totally familiar with your current financial situation and with your goals, only you can decide exactly what actions to take and when to do so. And, last, do not expect this book to cover every single investment area. I will discuss only the major areas. You will need to take my words and apply them to areas that are not discussed herein.

Within the broader investment perspective, the Y2K problem is more likely to be a bump in the road than a fork in the road. Accordingly, Y2K and its aftermath may well prove to be one of the most profitable buying opportunities in many years. I believe that Y2K should be hailed as an investment opportunity rather than feared as a potential destroyer of assets. Knowledge of effective investments will overcome the fear that is all too often prompted by ignorance.

The teachings of Zen tell us that "every front has a back." In other words, the millennium bug, while clearly threatening on the one hand, may have its positive side. In what follows I will discuss the positive as well as the negative aspects of Y2K and its aftermath. For those who believe that we can make lemonade from lemons, the new millennium will provide the best opportunities in many decades.

Jake Bernstein

ACKNOWLEDGMENTS

To write a book that has such far-reaching and serious implications is impossible without the dedicated assistance of qualified, motivated and competent helpers. To this end I owe considerable thanks to the following: Marilyn Kinney, my office manager and right-hand person, for organizing me in spite of my inherent disorganization;

Nan Barnum, my publication director, for the many hours she spent helping me pull together the details of this book; and

My family, for their patience while I rushed to finish my research and writing.

In particular, my son Elliott deserves special thanks for helping me with references and resources.

Ellen Coleman my editor at NYIF/Prentice Hall and Jackie Roulette, senior production editor were especially helpful in making the final product printworthy and as correct as possible.

Finally, a word of thanks to the many clients, friends and business associates who shared with me their opinions, fears and expectations about Y2K and its aftermath.

INTRODUCTION

A stock market "crash" is coming. The market boom of the 1990s will come to a climactic and dramatic end. The "millennium crash" (hereinafter referred to as "MC") is inevitable and

> Finally there came the awful day of reckoning for the bulls and the optimists and the wishful thinkers and those vast hordes that, dreading the pain of a small loss at the beginning, were about to suffer total amputation—without anesthetics.*
> —Edwin Lefevre, 1923

unavoidable. Although it may not come exactly on the first business day of the Year 2000, when it does come, its massive power will be incomprehensible as well as devastating. Investors, both private and institutional, will sell stocks in a frenzy that will most likely be precipitated by the *perception* of a problem rather than by any actual problem. What is in the minds and actions of the sellers will likely be exaggerated and exacerbated by minds brainwashed from fear. The crisis will happen seemingly without notice, gaining strength as it feeds on its own momentum.

As the market crisis deepens and intensifies, billions of U.S. dollars, Swiss francs, Japanese yen, German marks, pounds sterling in unrealized

---

* Lefevre, Edwin, *Reminiscence of a Stock Operator.* New York: John Wiley & Sons, Inc., 1923, 1994.

(paper) profits will be erased in a matter of hours or days. Investors and speculators will exit stocks globally and *en masse*. Sellers, failing to find willing buyers at high prices, will lower their offers until buyers emerge. But buyers will be few and far between. Under such conditions, an unprecedented selling panic may grip stock markets worldwide, threatening the very core of economic structures, market theories, political doctrines, governments, banks, investment firms and corporations. Gloom and doom sayers will echo "I told you so." Religious fanatics and cultists will claim the arrival of their long-awaited Armageddon. The anti-Christ will be disguised as an errant computer chip, blind and unable to read any dates beginning in the Year 2000. Survivalists who have prepared by retreating to a shack in the wilderness of Montana will rejoice in their *schadenfreude* (enjoyment obtained from the troubles of others) as they watch economic institutions and investors humbled before the power of the crash demon.

The Millennium Crash will leave its deep scars on the economic landscape for years to come. It will be the subject of popular books, magazine articles, scholarly works, documentaries, discussion groups, analyses and painful "I should have's." The excesses of market speculation in the 1990s will be corrected in a massive avalanche that few investors expect and for which fewer yet are prepared. You will remember where you were and what you were doing the day the MC hits, just as many of us remember where we were when President John F. Kennedy was assassinated.

But the MC will be qualitatively and quantitatively different from all market crashes that have come before. The global interdependence of markets, the very high level of stock prices, the hyper-anxious state of investors, the volatile inter-relationships of currencies, economies, computer systems and communications could well result in an international cataclysm that will spread like wildfire unless decisive and immediate actions are taken to halt the pandemic of fear. The best defense will be a strong offense. And the best offense will be a combination of knowledge, preparation and self-control.

The serious and lasting changes that are likely to occur in world economies, currency relationships and stock markets will not all be the result of what has been called the "millennium bug" (hereinafter referred to as "MB"); they will be the result of multiple facts, forces, patterns and events. In fact, later in this book I will pinpoint the confluence of seven major factors and forces as the key ingredients in a MC.

Alarm, Reality and Knowledge

While alarmists will be ready and primed for cataclysmic events to begin as the year 1999 draws to an end and the year 2000 begins, the MC will not necessarily begin on a given date. As far as I know, the start of the severe decline could begin as late as 2004, perhaps even later. It may begin as early as mid 1999. My view is a long-term one. I am not in the business of forecasting an exact date on which the MC will begin. I'll leave this task to the psychics, astrologers and newsletter writers who, in their hubris and delusions of grandeur, believe that they can pick exact dates and times for the start and end of long-term stock market moves.

Rather than give you dates, I will give you guidelines. Rather than exacerbate your fears, I will give you strategies to minimize them. Rather than give you only a few general ideas of how to prepare for Y2K and its fallout, I will present alternatives and scenarios designed to protect you.

Knowledge will be the deterrent to panic, and preparation will be the cure for fear. As 1999 ends and the new millennium comes, you will be bombarded by radio and television reports about the problems that are expected to develop. You will be assaulted and insulted by a plethora of articles, reports, books (like this one) and rumors about Y2K. My advice is to be calm, to be prepared, to be logical and above all, to evaluate events within the framework I will provide for you.

My Choice of Title

Before we dig more deeply into Y2K, I'd like to explain my choice of titles for this book. What exactly do I mean by the term *Millennium Crash*? Am I referring to a crash in the stock market, a crash in the U.S. economy, a crash in international markets and economies, or a brief reaction in an otherwise solid up move? Here is a simple and concise statement of what my title means:

I believe that as a result of a series of events, some related to Y2K computer problems, and others that are not directly related to these problems, world stock markets and economies are approaching a critical point in time. During this critical time the possibility of an "economic accident" is high. Such events are likely to be precipitated by Y2K problems some time in mid- to late 1999 and well into the year 2002. The MC could come as late as 2004.

Events that might have a relatively limited impact on markets and economies during less critical times may have a serious impact with far-reaching consequences during this vulnerable period of time. Hence, the prudent investor will take necessary precautions for what might—in the worst-case scenario—be a serious meltdown in financial institutions, government power and stock markets, or—in the best case—nothing more than an annoying blip on the upward course of economic growth. As you read my comments, the meaning of the title will become even clearer to you if you are still uncertain. So read on and see what I have to tell you. But above all, read with an open mind and attempt to learn from the patterns and relationships I will show you.

THE STAGE IS SET FOR THE FINAL ACT

For a variety of reasons, some logical, some mythical, but primarily psychological, humankind has often found it comforting to perpetuate a host of myths. Whether such myths are founded in fantasies passed on to us through the ages or based on experiences that are more contemporary, the fact remains that myth and superstition are more prevalent in modern times than many of us are willing to admit. Perhaps C. G. Jung was correct when he theorized the role of archetypal dream symbols in the so-called collective unconscious. We need not look too far to find evidence of such self-serving but scientifically unsubstantiated beliefs. Since the 1960s there has been a growing trend toward alternatives in virtually every aspect of life.

We have witnessed the burgeoning of alternative religions, alternative medicine, alternative schools, alternative lifestyles, alternative music and alternative societies. The "New Age," a time for questioning virtually every aspect of life and existence, has—strangely enough—fostered and facilitated the perpetuation of myth and superstition.

Whether it is anomie or ennui, many of us now seek to minimize our dependence on the trappings of external success in favor of our search for existential fulfillment. Our quest for meaning in life has prompted us to wander peculiar and varied paths. The search has given us modern-day alchemists, psychic channelers, television psychics, shamans, past life regression therapists, aura readers, empathic healers, angels, prophets and more. If you doubt my words, consider some of the best-selling books in recent years. You'll find angels, vampires, devils and prophets at the top of the list.

On late-night television you'll be exposed repeatedly to one of the most successful money-making promotional schemes ever: the various television psychic firms who offer you their "certified" psychics for only $3.99 per minute via a "900" telephone number. For this paltry sum you can chat one-on-one with a "live psychic" who will gladly advise you on matters of health, heart and wealth. Our thirst for answers is the demand that has created the supply.

I am not saying that there is no place for alternative medicine, alternate lifestyles or other so-called "New Age" ideas in our society. They have their place and if they get results, I'm entirely in favor of using them. I merely point out their proliferation as a sign of the times; as a sign that humankind in its search to find meaning in life has turned to a variety of answers in recent years, many of which reject the teachings of traditional science.

Such strong polarization revealing is a statement of how humankind now sees itself. We are a deeply divided lot, shaped so, in part by a loss of true meaning in life as basic social values have been circumvented by immediate gratification and "instantism." It is the inability to delay gratification and our growing dependence on technology that now threatens to push much of the world into the social and economic abyss. It is the fast pace of progress and the near exponential growth of technology that have created a serious dependency.

The existence of a global electronic community, whose birth and growth are a direct result of advances in computer technology and computer-based communications, should come as no surprise to future-oriented thinkers. While the Internet is now taken for granted, the idea of a global electronic community was proposed by Marshall McLuhan beginning in the late 1960s, and throughout the 1980s. His forecasts and theories were rejected by many of his peers. In fact, McLuhan was considered by his detractors to be a charlatan, a showman or a buffoon rather than a guru of electronic culture.

Nevertheless, McLuhan's ideas were prescient. Although couched in an idiosyncratic writing style, controversial, mystical and even untenable when first introduced, they have been vindicated by time.

His concepts threatened the existing power base of academia, a fact that was certain to cause McLuhan virtually instant rejection. His idea that context was more significant than content raised a hue and cry in academic circles.

Well before his assertion that the birth of a global electronic community was inevitable, McLuhan had, in fact, taken the next step. In a late 1960s interview with *Playboy* magazine, McLuhan stated as follows:

> The computer thus holds out the promise of a technologically engendered state of universal understanding and unity . . . the real use of the computer (is) . . . not to expedite marketing or solve technical problems but to speed the process of discovery and expedite terrestrial and eventually galactic environments and energies . . .*

While the electronic community that was so correctly predicted by McLuhan so many years ago has become a reality, it is still in its relative infancy. In this newborn state, content is still more significant to us than context. The greater goals of expediting "terrestrial . . . environments and energies" has not yet been achieved. Perhaps, the Y2K crisis will shock us into the realization that we have not yet reached a state of perfection in computer technology and communications and that new challenges await us with each new step that technology takes. Even if the MC fails to cause any significant problems, the anticipation and *possibility* of a crisis should serve as a valuable lesson to us. Yet, as I write these words, the seeds of a possible economic catastrophe have been sown and now await either harvest or eradication.

Acting as a strong aggravating factor in the equation for economic disease is the increasingly tenuous role of government and politics on business and society. As Rees-Moog and Davidson have so correctly pointed out in their forward-thinking book, *The Sovereign Individual,* governments and politicians the world over are beginning to lose their vise-like grip on society. As the Internet has allowed creation of a global village, people have been given the opportunity to transact international commerce instantly, without travel and, at times, entirely outside the scepter of government surveillance. Anyone who feels alienated by efforts of government to control their rights can leave their coun-

---

* McLuhan, Eric, and Zingrone, Frank, *Essential McLuhan.* New York: Basic Books, 1995. p. 262.

try and still conduct business as well as many personal affairs via the Internet. Internet connectivity can serve as the sole source of commerce and communication with clients. Face-to-face meetings are no longer necessary.

Clearly this poses a threat to the government power base. The ability to tax, regulate, abuse and control citizens is rapidly diminishing. Realization of this power loss has prompted governments to take hostile and often unwarranted action against those whom it perceives as threats to its power base. It is not surprising, therefore, that Bill Gates, the quintessential computer giant and symbolic leader of computer power, was singled out as a target for U.S. government investigation.

Politicians are a dying breed. Their techniques of reaching and influencing the public are effete. Their thinking is often archaic, out of touch with the technological realities. They rarely represent the will of the people. Today's political institutions are grossly inefficient, wasteful, corrupt, self-serving and cloaked in favoritism. Political in-fighting has increased as big government fish attempt to devour smaller fish, all at the expense of the taxpayer. There have been and will continue to be numerous political witch hunts, all costing the public billions of dollars. And for what purpose? For the same reason that a bully seeks to climb to the top of the hill in the schoolyard—for control and power.

Instant worldwide communications via telephone and Internet are slowly but most surely eroding government power bases throughout the world. News travels worldwide within seconds of its occurrence. People all over the world are now more informed, more educated, more computer savvy, more verbal, more vocal and more anti–big-government than ever before.

What does all of this have to do with Y2K? I believe that any disruption in computer communications via Internet can aggravate an already intense global state of anxiety. Without their e-mail, chat rooms and news boards, global uncertainty could very well lead to panic. Without the ability to conduct reliable, efficient and prompt electronic commerce the many Internet vendors will come to a complete standstill. The speculative frenzy that boosted the stock of Internet-based sellers such as Amazon.com, Broadcast.com and Books-a-Million could well turn into a selling frenzy that causes their stock to crash. But such reactions may prove to be only the tip of the MC iceberg.

Have It Now—Get It Now—Buy It Now

Immediacy reigns supreme in the 1990s. You can log on to the Internet and within seconds you can see world news, download music and video clips, "chat" with people you've never met, post bulletins in newsgroups, buy books, videos or CDs for delivery the next day, find a new or used car, and even buy and download software instantly. For those who seek to satisfy their sexual desires, no matter what time of day, thousands of "porn" web sites are available for instant access at the mere entry of a credit card number. Whether you're a peeping tom interested in "hidden locker room cam" or a submissive looking for a good disciplining from an experienced dominatrix, you can get it now on the Net.

On the more pragmatic side of things, you can trade stocks online with instant electronic order entry, you can check your bank balance, transfer funds or donate money to your favorite charity. If none of this happens fast enough for you with a 56K modem, you can get yourself an ISDN high-speed connection or a super-fast T1 line or a variety of even faster alternatives. And you can enjoy all of these on your new incredibly fast 400-megahertz PIII computer that sports an ultra-fast 24X CD/ROM drive with a fast access internal hard drive. Of course your pleasure and speed of processing can be increased with a few hundred megabytes of 9-nanosecond memory chips and a voice recognition package designed to speed up inputs. And you can relax in style while you do all of this on new office furniture you don't have to make payments on until 12 months from now, and you can do so at the low, low finance rate of 5 percent, guaranteed.

In our world of the late 1990s, speed has pervaded virtually every aspect of life. Stocks move up and down faster than ever before. News travels across the world instantly via the Internet. It is precisely this speed that can serve as devil or angel. On the one hand, having instant access allows us to operate more efficiently and therefore to achieve more and to enjoy more of the relatively short span of time we have on this earth. On the other hand, speed can be deleterious, exacerbating panic. Where we once had the luxury of taking days or even weeks to make decisions that affect our personal and financial welfare, it seems that we now have only days or even minutes to achieve the same result.

For many years, investors could sit methodically in front of their charts or newspapers pondering earnings or chart formations, reading about company management or analyzing stock and economic trends prior to making a financial commitment in a given stock or mutual fund. Now, with stock market swings so fast and furious, investors and money managers must act almost immediately in order to either take advantage of an opportunity or to avoid a loss.

In addition, the speed of Internet communications allows investors the world over to share information almost immediately via news groups and web sites. Recommendations to buy or sell given stocks or commodities can reach thousands of people at the same time. In the past such recommendations could only be made available via postal mail delivery, FAX, telephone or TELEX, none of which were so efficient or inexpensive as Internet delivery. Information can either promote intelligent and logical decision making or it can prompt panic reactions. When someone yells "fire" in a crowded theater, the result is often panic and death as a stampede ensues. On the other hand, an orderly and controlled exit from the burning theater results in minimal loss of life or injury.

In many respects the financial markets are like a crowded theater. The markets are crowded with investors of all types. We've got mutual fund managers, pension fund managers, bank traders, individual investors, investment clubs, speculators, hedge fund managers, day traders and more. And every single one of them has the same goal— to make money. Since late 1987, the start of the strongest bull market in history, the U.S. stock market has been moving higher. As prices have moved steadily up ignoring bad news and feeding on good news, investors have become increasingly spoiled. They have assumed that the feeding frenzy will continue indefinitely, that their money will continue to grow, that picking winning stocks is relatively easy, that the future is bright and that a falling market will not last too long.

These attitudes have been developed and perpetuated by the market itself. In relation to the market conditions of the late 1990s, they are not unrealistic attitudes. By the time you read this book, conditions may have changed, but if they have, they likely have followed the course that I outline in these pages. Even if world stock markets have declined and find themselves in downward trends, the possibility of a steep decline during already declining markets is still a stark reality.

By now you may be asking yourself why my focus is on the stock market. The answer is simple. Like it or not, the direction of stock prices is a key indicator of economic health. A rising stock market typically indicates a healthy economy whereas a falling stock market tends to indicate an ailing economy. What concerns me most about the Y2K crisis is how the stock market will act in the face of panicked selling prompted by the growing need to act immediately upon news. I will clarify precisely what I mean by this and how panic could easily be transformed into a market decline of dire consequences; a decline that could easily rival the market crashes of 1929 and 1987.

For those of us who are prepared, a decline in stock prices could well serve as an opportunity to generate significant short-term profits. Do you bristle at the thought of making money when panic reigns? Do you feel that your profits will be at the expense of other people's suffering? If so, I suggest you abandon those thoughts. Investors who are savvy and forward thinking are to be rewarded for their efforts. If we are prepared for the MC and if we profit, then we are entitled to those profits. We will not have caused the financial panic. Hence, there is no need to feel guilty. It is the lack of preparation, lack of self-control, ignorance and perhaps even stupidity of others that will contribute to, and perhaps aggravate, a possible millennium market panic. Losses will be the direct consequence of their poor preparation. If we prepare correctly and adequately, then we will emerge from the fire unscathed at the very least and more wealthy at the very best. Yet, I emphasize that we will do so not at the expense of others but rather as a reward for our efforts.

Economic Yin and Yang: Cycles of Boom and Bust

Cycles of boom and bust are not new to world economies or to stock markets. There have been at least six major boom-and-bust cycles in America since the 1700s and many more minor cycles. A study of economic history underscores the inescapable fact that markets and economies breathe in and must eventually breathe out. Markets rise and fall, often in relatively predictable rhythms. When markets are in an upward trend, optimism reigns supreme. Politicians are elated, the public is happy, investment managers are proud and retirees find little to complain about as long as their money has been wisely invested.

Ultimately, as the momentum of good times grows, optimism reaches a state of euphoria that frequently culminates in a climactic buying surge. More often than not, such extreme levels of buying and optimism correlate closely with an end to the period of "boom." Whereas the future looked bright during the boom phase, and perhaps brightest at its peak, events and investor psychology soon changes with the changing tide of the markets and the economy.

When the cycle of "bust" begins, optimism is still high. Shortly after a few severe declines in the stock market and a few negative indications from government, pessimism takes hold. Markets decline, the economy contracts and politicians fear for their jobs. The public is angry, shocked and frustrated that the markets are declining. Money managers are fearful of speculative stocks, seeking instead conservative investments for their clients. Retirees are frustrated as they watch the value of their stock portfolios erode almost daily. Pessimism begets more pessimism until the stock market and the overall economy plunge even lower in a last gasp of selling. At times, however, only a whimper and not a bang characterize the end of a "bust" phase. Occasionally, a new boom cycle is born of a humble beginning following a period of stagnation, one during which there is relatively little movement as markets and economies gather energy for the coming upward phase.

The Role and Ability of Governments

Investors tend to have considerable faith in the ability of governments to control boom-and-bust cycles. After all, governments can control the supply of money, interest rates, the degree of market speculation, fiscal policies that affect supply and demand, credits and loans to foreign countries and a host of other less significant variables. All of these, when combined, can exert a marked effect on the direction of stocks, other investments and the general economy.

Students of American history point to the fact that economic depressions during the terms of Presidents Van Buren, Buchanan, Grant, Cleveland, Theodore Roosevelt and Woodrow Wilson were either allowed to occur as a result of the government's lack of interest, or exacerbated by the fact that none of these administrations took an active role in avoiding or alleviating them. On the other hand, the Hoover administration parted with tradition, taking an active role in economic policies designed to remediate the severe effects of the Great Depression. This was a turning point in the role of government with regard to economic health, safety and welfare.

Today government is actively involved in facilitating economic growth, controlling inflationary pressures, stimulating the economy when necessary and, one hopes, minimizing the effects of boom-and-bust cycles. The prevailing opinion among investors is that the government not only has a large arsenal of weapons to use in the fight against economic extremes, but also that the weapons will work when they are needed. This, of course, remains to be seen.

Predictability of Boom-and-Bust Cycles

The cycles of boom and bust in free world economies are not nearly so predictable as the oscillations of planets, the motion of electrons or the coming and going of the seasons. However, they do have their internal and external patterns, which, within a reasonable degree of variation, have a lengthy history of repetition. A number of well-respected classical economists, including such notables as Joseph Schumpeter, recognized this fact, incorporating it into their theories of prices and economics. Some of these cyclical patterns are highly important in the long-term patterns of prices and markets in the U.S. economy. Many of them will be discussed later in this book.

"GOOD GUYS" VS. "BAD GUYS"

Stock and commodity price history in America reads like a drama of "good guys" vs. "bad guys." The good guys in this high stakes economic thriller are the bulls, the optimists, those who feel that markets will rise forever with only minor setbacks along the way. They are the politicians who have "worked hard" to improve the lot of their constituents. They are the mutual fund managers who have practiced their analytical skills, choosing the best stocks that money can buy. And they are the bankers who, in their endless beneficence, have loaned money to individuals and businesses, thereby allowing them to profit in a growing economy.

In their Panglossian view, all is for the best in the best of all possible markets. Declines are seen as "corrections." Bad news is considered an opportunity to buy more stocks. "Buy high and sell higher" is one of their credos. "Buy low and sell high" is their theme song. Government attempts to control the economy from excessive growth is a necessary but bitter pill to swallow; yet government in this phase of growth is considered a necessary evil. Yes, even the government is seen favorably when the economy is healthy and stocks are rising.

Those who are cautious, pessimistic or bearish are the bad guys. They are often labeled as the "gloom and doomers." Their view is that upward price moves are temporary and that sooner or later markets will crash at the first whisper of bad news. In their pessimistic view, all progress is temporary. They view economic statistics as lies perpetuated by a government whose sole purpose is to hide the economic truth from the people they were elected to serve. They promote "hard money" investments as a hedge against the eventual collapse of stocks, systems and government.

The good guys and bad guys are not organized into definitive camps, clubs or groups, however; they are found everywhere. Every nation, every economy, every political party and every school of economic theory has its share of the "yin and yang." While there are elements of truth in each camp, the actual truth is likely to be found somewhere in the middle. A good guy can become a bad guy almost instantly depending upon his or her view of the markets and the economy. Conversely, changing his or her opinions from negative to positive can redeem a bad guy. Clearly, at the peak of a market and at the top of an economic cycle good guys substantially outnumber bad guys. At the end of an economic cycle or declining market bad guys are in the majority while good guys are either afraid to come out of the closet, or they parade as bay guys with a good-guy mentality.

A LIFE OF THEIR OWN

The more we learn about markets and economies, the more we realize that they have a life of their own. They are born, often from the ashes of a previously moribund economy; they grow slowly at first.

They continue their growth until they reach a crest, and then they begin their decline. Their fall is at first unnoticeable, perhaps even insipid. However, as the decline continues it gains momentum under the forces of economic gravity and eventually a rapid decline ensues. Ultimately the decline slows, a period of consolidation follows and a bottom is eventually reached.

The life cycle of markets and economies follow the same general phases although the ramifications of each phase are different. Clearly a change in the economic trend can have a domino effect on all sectors of the economy, including the stock and commodity markets. Yet, it is also possible for the stock and commodity markets to affect the economic trend in certain circumstances. This "chicken or egg" question has long been a source of controversy among economists, market technicians, traders, investors, market analysts, bankers and government. The ultimate answer will never be known since no market or economy functions in a vacuum. An excess of negative economic news can put fear into the hearts of investors and investment managers. Their attitudes can change as a result of perceived fundamentals which may prompt them to sell. Mass negative perceptions may result in an avalanche of selling that will, in turn, cause security prices to decline.

On the other hand, the opposite is also possible: The overall economic outlook may be positive, but concerted selling of stocks by large investors and traders can reverberate throughout the economy, causing investors to avoid stocks, cut back on spending and thereby affect the overall economy. Clearly the inter-relationships of all economic sectors, emotion, stock market trends, international and domestic news, all operate in a complex fashion maintaining an often delicate balance, a balance that can be upset by a variety of influences.

Yesterday, Today and Tomorrow

The present stock market rally started in the early 1980s. On a very broad scale, plotting stock trends using a logarithmic measure, the rally actually began in 1932 following the Great Depression. There have been only a handful of significant declines since the start of the greatest bull market in history. Beginning in 1995 the U.S. stock market started a near vertical acceleration. While there are numerous comparisons between the current U.S. stock market and the stock market of the 1920s, there are more differences than similarities.

Hence, a simple conclusion that the U.S. stock market is destined to crash based on similarities between the current market and the pre-1929 crash market alone is likely to be wrong as well as unrealistic. There are, however, other causes for concern; causes that are global, inter-related and considerably more significant than any single aspect of the U.S. and/or world economies of the 1920s.

Paper Millionaires

The largest bull market in U.S. history has created more paper millionaires than any stock market rally heretofore, and has attracted more investment dollars into mutual funds than ever before. This rally has lulled investors into a false sense of security.

Consider the following questions that should be on the minds of all investors:

- Are the seeds now sown for a cataclysmic change in economic trends and stock market direction?
- Will stock markets throughout the world crash as a result of excessive speculation, or will they fall due to panic precipitated by serious problems in the financial and technological infrastructure of business and government because of the Year 2000 bug?
- Will the change in trend catch most professional money managers unprepared or with low cash reserves?
- Will the new breed of paper millionaires created by a soaring stock market be transformed into a new class of paupers virtually overnight?
- Will a significant downward reversal in world stock markets precipitate a chain reaction of bank failures?
- Will the U.S. Federal Reserve raise interest rates sharply in order to curb excessive speculation prior to a millennium crash, or will they act as a reaction to such a crisis?
- Is it possible that the U.S. Federal Reserve will actually lower interest rates in anticipation of stock market problems?

- Will another wave of negative economic events in the Asian economies cause a chain reaction in world markets?

- Could a default by some South American countries be the trigger for a financial panic and stock market decline that will also be exacerbated by a millennium crisis?

- Will many world economies collapse as a result of the above?

- Will business disruption in the infrastructure resulting from Millennium Bug computer problems prompt a chain reaction of cataclysmic economic events?

- How can the average investor prepare for what may develop over the next few years?

- What precedent is there to the protective strategies that are frequently recommended? Will they work again?

- Is a stock market crash imminent?

- Are there ways to profit from a possible decline?

- Will interest rates skyrocket?

- How will governments react to imminent Y2K problems?

- Who will be prepared to deal with the Y2K problem?

- Who stands to get hurt most from a Y2K panic? Who least?

These are only a few of the questions this book will answer. The facts are plain, simple and obvious, and the conclusions are reasonable. A significant decline in world stock markets is coming and with that decline, economic concerns may also develop. The crisis may be upon us sooner than many of us believe and it will be more violent than many of us believe. Rather than a mere decline in one stock market, the change in market direction will impact all free world stock markets and economies. While there are many positive aspects to a global economy, this is the dark side, the curse of a global economy.

More than ever before, a sneeze in Tokyo has the potential to cause a headache in London, a knee jerk in Paris, a stomach ache in Milan and a seizure in the United States. This is the price that we pay as members of the global economy; and it is a dear price indeed. But, as always, knowledge will be power. This book will give you the knowledge to anticipate, to extract meaning from apparent madness and to act in advance rather than react in panic when the financial bomb hits.

Finally, it is important to remember that you need not be a financial wizard or market analyst to see what is happening and what will happen. To realize what the new millennium holds in store, not only in terms of stock markets and economies worldwide, but for your personal welfare and safety, does not require a degree in rocket science. The importance of what J. Peter Steidlmayer has defined as "market generated information" cannot be ignored or underestimated.

> Thus, today we have two forms of knowledge: that which comes directly as a result of one's own observations of reality, and that which comes from a derivative source such as a teacher, a book, a television show or movie, etc. The first form was all that man had prior to the introduction of sophisticated forms of communication. The second form modern man relies on heavily, often at the expense of being correct and accurate.*

Market-generated information comes to us directly from markets. It is not information that has been analyzed or interpreted to the point of obfuscation. The inevitable approach of the MB provides market analysts and commentators the opportunity to interpret and examine reality in terms of their pet theories and systems. I believe that in the final analysis, we will be served best by close attention to information generated by markets and the economic realities than by interpretations that are twice or thrice removed from actual events. The well-worn aphorism "keep it simple, stupid" (KISS) will likely serve you better come Y2K and its aftermath, than any complex theory of waves, chart patterns or artificial intelligence and neural network systems. I include here my own theories. This is why I have kept my theoretical and interpretive meandering to a minimum while focusing on pragmatics and the lessons of history.

---

* Steidlmayer, J. P., and Koy, K., *Markets and Market Logic.* Chicago: Porcupine Press, 1986. p. 2.

THE BULL THAT WOULDN'T STOP–OR WILL IT?

The U.S. stock market as measured by the Dow Jones Industrial Average (DJIA) has enjoyed a steady upward acceleration since early 1995. In January of that year the average was in the 3850 area. By the end of 1995 the DJIA sat at 5117. The rally had been spectacular, surprising even the most optimistic analysts and forecasters. The year 1996 began slowly as prices retreated from their 1995 gains. However, by July 1996 a low was in place for the year. Prices once again shot higher to end the year at a new record of 6448. The market had clearly surpassed the expectations of the most raging bulls, yet it showed no definitive signs, technically or fundamentally, of stopping. The up-move was a continuation of a virtually uninterrupted trend that started after the Crash of 1987. And the Crash of 1987 was the first major market decline in many years.

> Shares of Broadcast.com Inc., an unprofitable provider of audio and video programming over the Internet, on Friday posted the largest first-day gain of any sizable initial public offering this decade . . . rocketing from their offering price of $18 to close at $62.75, a gain of 249 percent . . . Friday's frenzied trading left the company with a market capitalization of $1.06 billion.
> —*The Wall Street Journal,* July 20, 1998

Although the market was on a strong upward course, there were no signs that the general public or the small investor was too optimistic. Investment professionals and larger traders took this as a generally positive sign. As long as optimism did not rule among smaller investors, and as long as there was an orderly tone to stock market declines, it was likely that prices would move still higher. And they did. The DJIA began 1997 at 6453. Following several months of consolidation, the market made a new all-time high in August of that year at an unbelievable 8299, more than doubling its January 1995 reading. But the rally wasn't over yet!

The year 1998 started on an unsteady footing following the 1997 all-time high. However, by the end of February the market sat at a new all-time high of 8545. There was no stopping the greatest bull market in history. No matter what the news, no matter what the fundamentals and no matter what negatives the pessimists trotted out, the market pushed ever higher. It was a *fait accompli* the 10,000 level was destined to be "cracked" in 1999. And it was!

As still another nail in the coffin of the bears, market technicians pointed out the fact that the Dow Jones Utilities Stock Average (DJU) had also made a new all-time high and remained strong. This was a positive indication inasmuch as these stocks are interest-rate sensitive. If utilities need to borrow money at high rates, their profits suffer. However, if the cost of money is low, their profits will improve and their stock will be attractive. Concerns over a rise in interest rates might inhibit savvy investors and institutions from buying utility stocks, which could be a harbinger of trouble for the market, but there were no indications from the U.S. Federal Reserve that interest rates would be raised.

Amazing Gains Not Uncommon

The ten pure Internet companies whose stock was offered to the public in 1998 showed an average gain of 110 percent by July 1998, with some stocks having gained well over 200 percent. Excite Inc. shares rose from a low of under $5 per share in mid-1997 to a high of over $55 per share in July 1998. Having risen a mere 500 percent in 11 months, Excite was one of the tame Internet stocks. America Online Inc., whose future was uncertain in mid-1997, rallied from about $34 per share to about $140 by late July 1998.

Shares of Amazon.com, the Internet bookseller, rose from under $10 per share in August of 1997 to over $140 per share in July of 1998, posting a gain of 164 percent from June 8, 1998 through July 10, 1998. While the rise was spectacular, some might consider it clearly insane since Amazon.com was generating no profits at the time, on an estimated 1998 revenue of over $663 million!

Rampant speculation in Internet stocks was merely one aspect of the 1998 buying frenzy. And 1999 witnessed even more spectacular gains in Internet-related shares. While the stocks of solid, well-established companies such as UAL Incorporated (the parent company of United Airlines) sold at $88 per share, the stock of startup Internet companies such as Yahoo! were trading at over $200 per share. Speculation was indeed running rampant; however, it had not yet reached the degree of insanity that has typically characterized major market and economic peaks.

FUTURES MARKETS: TAME BY COMPARISON

By ironic contrast, the futures markets, once considered the most speculative of all speculations (perhaps other than oil exploration), were plodding along with relatively minor moves daily. In fact, investors seemed uninterested in futures trading (other than stock index and Treasury bond futures trading), as the once hot futures markets of the 1970s and 1980s contracted severely. Why speculate in futures when stocks offered a more readily understandable opportunity with large potential as trading vehicles?

But the big bull market of the 1990s is not an isolated example of speculation. Speculative tops have been made in many markets throughout history. It is tempting, of course, to draw a comparison between the bull market top of 1929 and the subsequent crash, and the bull market of the 1990s. While there are some comparisons, every market has a life of its own and is driven by its own set of facts, fantasies and fundamentals. In this book I will outline for you the various stages of markets so that you may determine the stage of any market in a stock, commodity or investment.

The simple fact is that most markets begin with a crawl, progress to a walk, develop into a run and end with frenzy. Rampant speculation and crashes are as much a part of every growth cycle in every market economy as slow and steady growth. It is the nature of all things human to engage in excesses. We will examine some of these excesses and compare them to the events that are developing as we approach the Year 2000, as well as to those that are due to develop until approximately the year 2005.

Danger in Paradise

The bull continued to run, yet all was not well in paradise. Those who were proponents of the Dow Theory expressed concern that the Dow Jones Transportation Stock Index (DJT) failed to follow the trends and the new all-time highs in the DJIA and DJU averages. Figure 1.1 shows the divergent relationship. If transportation stocks were not following the general market rise, it could indicate that demand for goods was slowing down, that travel was on the decline and that the ultimate result would be a decrease in corporate profits. Failure of the DJT to follow the general stock market to new highs was considered a classical sell signal according to leading Dow Theory watchers.

As you can see from an examination of Figure 1.1, in early July of 1998 the DJI (the top half of the illustration) reached a new all-time peak. At the same time, however, the DJT (the bottom half) failed to reach a new all-time peak. This was considered a negative factor, which was expected to lead to a severe decline. Many suspected that this might very well be the end of the biggest bull market in history, but, as you can see, following a drop from the all-time high in July 1998, the market resumed its upward path, much to the surprise of the "experts," the gloom and doom sayers, and the crash predictors. And the trend has moved even higher as prices made new all-time highs in early 1999.

When the predicted crash failed to happen, people began to wonder if this bull market was truly unstoppable. The key questions that most people ask are how long will the rally last, how high will the market go and how severe will the coming decline be. But these are specifics that are not necessarily important in the long run. We all want to know the future of markets, trends and economies. Our desire to know is inspired primarily by two factors—the quest for profit and the need to protect one's assets. I believe that, given valid and effective tools, you will be able to discern major changes in markets and economic trends on your own. The key to doing so effectively will be to develop alternatives and strategic plans. This will be an important

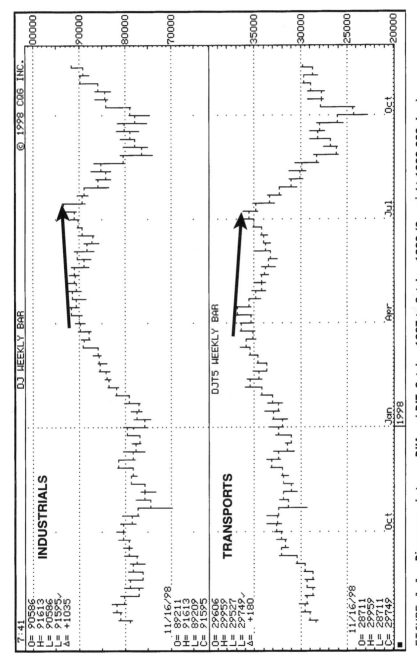

FIGURE 1.1 Divergence between DJIA and DJT, October 1997 to October 1998 (Copyright 1998 CQG, Inc.)

aspect of the chapters that follow. Yes, there is "danger in paradise" but what will come of it? How will it be resolved? Will danger become yet another major investment opportunity or will it end as a stock market crash, inspired by Y2K problems?

INTEREST RATES, PEACE AND PETROLEUM

Interest rates remain low in the late 1990s. The U.S. Federal Reserve system, in its wisdom, has not been concerned about excessive economic growth. Other than a few continuing flare-ups in the Middle East, the international political situation has been fairly stable. Oil prices have remained at their lowest levels in over 10 years. Overall employment, although high and potentially an inflationary concern, seemed to be peaking. There were indications that peak employment levels were receding somewhat, which was a positive indication since it suggested that inflation resulting from excessive consumer spending was not an immediate concern.

Strength in the U.S. market was reflected in stock markets the world over with the exception of Asia. The London FTSE100 stock average, which was at approximately 1584 in November of 1987, had rallied to over 6000 by mid-1998, a spectacular rise. The German DAX stock index was at a low of 1310 in early 1991. By July 1998 the index was at a new record of over 6070, in the midst of a near vertical rise for 1998 (Figure 1.2). And the CAC-40, Paris stock index was at 4370 in July of 1998. In March of 1995 the Paris index was at a low point of 1719. Although the Asian situation remained a cause for concern, investors were encouraged by how well stock markets in Europe and North America responded to the crisis. The feeling that we in the West were relatively immune from Asian crises was still another bullish consideration.

Clearly, investors, mutual fund managers, the government, stockbrokers and investment newsletter writers were elated at the persistence and magnitude of the rallies. The price of Standard and Poor's 500 (S&P) futures in Chicago had reached such high levels that traders expressed concerns about their ability to cope with the large margin requirements. Additionally, the high margin on S&P futures dissuaded retail customers from speculating in this high-risk market.

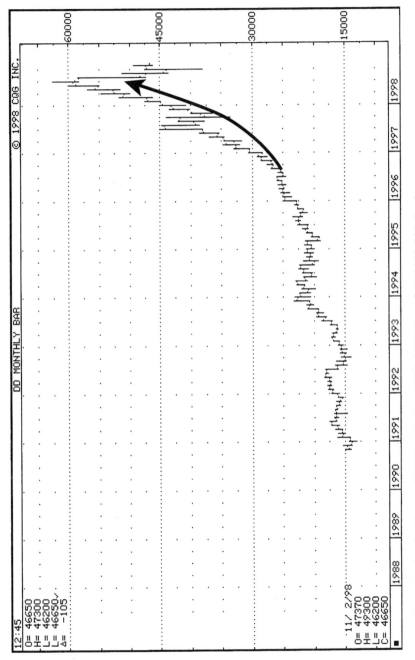

FIGURE 1.2 Soaring German DAX Stock Index, 1990–1998 (Copyright 1998 CQG, Inc.)

Pit brokers were concerned about decreased liquidity. In response to this concern the Chicago Mercantile Exchange, home of S&P futures trading, effectively split the contract two for one, allowing more traders to participate in the speculative game. Furthermore, a new S&P contract was offered on a one-tenth size basis. Called the "E-Mini," this contract is traded entirely on an electronic basis free from the influence of pit brokers. The usually stodgy and conservative Chicago Board of Trade (CBOT), in order to meet the growing speculative demand in stock index futures, introduced their Dow Jones Futures contract. After sitting idly by for years as the Chicago Mercantile Exchange led the world in stock index futures trading, the CBOT—after introducing an essentially failed Major Market Index—finally achieved a minor victory with their Dow contract.

Futures trading in essential agricultural commodities such as grains, soybeans and livestock declined as trading in stock index futures remained active. In June of 1998 approximately 20,000 Dow futures contracts were being traded daily. S&P futures trading volume was running at about 250,000 contracts daily. In both cases a large portion of the daily trading volume was purely within the day timeframe and entirely speculative.

COMMODITY EXCHANGE MEMBERSHIP PRICES "CRASH": FOREBODING

As trading volume in basic commodities decreased, the price of memberships at the Chicago Board of Trade and the Chicago Mercantile Exchange (the two largest futures exchanges in the world) began a steep decline. The price decline was exacerbated by the introduction of electronic trading that would eventually replace pit brokers who filled orders. Yet the two major U.S. exchanges were caught between a computer and a hard place. The London International Financial Futures Exchange (LIFFE) in a relatively short period of time had become the world's third largest exchange by innovative marketing, efficient order processing, supportive government trading regulations and the use of electronic trading.

Meanwhile, a restrictive regulatory climate in the United States along with the slow moving and self-serving leadership at the Chicago exchanges combined to cause severe problems for pit brokers. The problem was clear: If the floor broker was eliminated from the equation by the introduction of purely electronic trading, then the bread and butter of floor trader income would be lost. Hence, memberships might not offer an advantage since the pit broker could no longer "shave" points on transactions. The broker would lose the "edge" since electronic trading would dispense entirely with the so-called "open outcry" system.

Clearly, this was a clash of the old and the new. Pit brokers at the Chicago Board of Trade had enjoyed a virtual monopoly on the grain futures markets since the late 1800s. Despite the known fact that most floor brokers made their money on small increments as they sold to the public after buying at lower prices (and vice versa), the system continued since it was felt that the floor broker had a mandate to "make a market," providing liquidity. Yet, the market crash of 1987 proved that floor brokers were not capable of doing an efficient job in the face of severe panic and market crisis.

In an effort to keep pace with the LIFFE, electronic trading was approved by several U.S. exchanges. While it was hard to swallow, it was necessary nonetheless. This brings me finally to the point. By the year 2002, many markets in the United States will be traded on an entirely electronic basis. Although some markets will remain "open outcry" systems that favor floor brokers, I believe that markets such as currency futures, Treasury bonds, petroleum futures and stock index futures will be primarily electronic markets. Hence, they will be vulnerable to the Y2K problem as well as to difficulties that may develop if and when a panic comes. The electronic system could easily fail. And if it does, the result may well be a death knell not only to futures exchanges who are still not sufficiently prepared, but also to the finances of futures speculators who depend on reliable market information as well as accurate quotations and prompt order executions. Should exchanges fail to deliver in the event of a Y2K panic, the results could well be disastrous inasmuch as many stock market fund managers hedge their risk in stocks by trading stock index futures.

ANOTHER HIGH REACHED

In mid-July of 1998, U.S. stocks reached yet another all-time high as the DJIA hit 9305. The fact that rallies were persistent and resistant to negative news was the most valid reason for joy in the investment community. There seemed to be little, if any, news that could change the direction of the stock markets in North America or in Europe. Possibly, an unexpected rise in U.S. interest rates could be a negative. But if the increase was minimal and temporary, then the DJIA might set back just a bit before marching onward and upward to the 10,000 mark or much higher.

As the rally continued, those who had accumulated stock in pension plans through their many years of employment at large companies found themselves slowly but surely becoming wealthier with each passing month. Within a few years a plethora of paper millionaires had been created. As the rally continued, mutual fund sales soared as investors poured billions into the hands of professional money managers, many of whom were consistently beating the market. This added to their credibility and attracted still more capital in spite of the record high stock market averages.

Yet, was it such a great feat to beat a market that refused to give up? Clearly, anyone who was a proponent and practitioner of the "buy and hold" philosophy did well, as did those who adhered to the "buy on bad news in a bull market" also did well. Who lost? Those who were closed out of their long positions on the way up lost potential profits and, of course, short sellers lost unless they were nimble and able to grab quick profits during the relatively few market declines. Finally, those who failed to participate in the greatest of all bull markets lost by failing to accumulate potential profits.

The key considerations in evaluating the future of the U.S. and European stock markets are much deeper than simply determining who the consistent winners in this fantastic bubble are.

The key questions are:

- Who will get to keep their paper profits?
- Who will own too much stock when the top comes?
- Who will buy stock from the sellers?
- How will the mutual funds that own massive amounts of stock "unload" it in an orderly fashion?
- How, when and why will the so-called "Millennium Bug" affect the stock markets?
- Is it possible that there will be no significant Y2K market reaction at all?

- Who will be left holding the bag as buyers at or near the top of the market sell? And,

- What are the potential economic, social and political ramifications of a significant market top and a lengthy decline?

While the answers to these questions may seem rather obvious in the cold analytical light of day, a less logical view, one inspired by extreme optimism, tends to obscure facts and causes investors to view fictions as realities. Expectations become facts and wishes become certainties. In order to find cogent and valid replies to these nagging and pertinent questions, let's examine a few aspects of stock market behavior that will shed light on the subject.

STOCK MARKET CYCLES

It has been hypothesized that all free world economies move in long-wave cyclical patterns, and it has been shown that stock and commodity prices also move in cyclical patterns. The names most closely associated with cyclical theories are economists Joseph Schumpeter, N. D. Kondratieff and Jay W. Forrester. Their theories differ, but their conclusions are generally similar. The study of stock market cycles has been an ongoing project of The Foundation for the Study of Cycles. The foundation has identified many cycles in stock prices. The implications of these patterns will be discussed in later chapters.

One important conclusion is that no market, no economy, no individual stock, no commodity, no interest rate measure and no real estate market moves higher forever. This does not mean that investors are urged to take action in anticipation of a change in trend. Rather, it means that at certain times in the lifespan of a market trend, investors should watch for signs and symptoms that accompany or closely correlate with a change in market direction. Since cyclical patterns are not perfectly symmetrical or totally predictable, additional confirming measures must be used.

When peaks develop in markets and economies, experts offer many explanations for the top and ensuing decline. Frequently such tops come as a "surprise" to many individuals. In some cases even governments and economists are taken by surprise. Yet, close study of the factors and forces preceding such events often reveals well in advance that there is danger of a major change in direction. There is rarely one specific factor that prompts the decline. Most often a multiplicity of events, forces and factors are part of the total picture. When we think of the Stock Market Crash of 1929, for example, we tend to believe that it was caused by excessive speculation on low margin. In fact, this was only one cause. At least five additional factors contributed to the Crash of 1929 and the subsequent Great Depression.

If and when the current stock market begins its decline, and if the economy follows suit, rest assured that although the MB and Y2K crisis may be blamed for "causing" the decline, this will not, in fact, be the case. As the millennium draws to an end there are several conditions and forces that will factor into the overall cause for a decline. It is not possible to parse out any one aspect and assign full blame to it. Yet the media may see things differently at first. Eventually, with the passage of time, history will record the facts leading up to and contributing to a millennium market crash and economic contraction fully and accurately.

Nine Horsemen of the Economic Apocalypse

I believe there are nine factors that may all act in unison or in close contiguity to bring about a significant market top and potentially lengthy economic contraction in many capitalist economies:

1. The Millennium Bug and its potentially disruptive impact on electronic commerce, banking, national and international financial dealings and the infrastructure of municipalities throughout the world

2. Panic by small investors unable to resist an initial market decline and the onslaught of seemingly negative news

3. Selling of stocks by pension funds, banks and mutual funds

4. Major currency disruptions, economic disruptions and in-fighting in European countries as a consequence of the unified European currency

5. A cyclical peak in the four-year U.S. stock market cycle

6. A cyclical bottom in the 54-year interest rate cycle

7. Potential loan defaults by various South American countries

8. A major low in commodity prices, resulting in inflationary pressures that will force governments to react by raising interest rates, and

9. Panic liquidation of highly speculative stocks when the Internet stock bubble bursts

There may be a variety of additional factors that could contribute to or even exacerbate these nine. Among them I include the possibility of increased terrorism, another Asian financial crisis, and/or a Mid-East War.

Learn the Signs

Although market technicians and investment professionals make their living by timing changes in market trends, their work is by no means arcane or difficult to understand. Some technicians go to considerable lengths in order to couch their work in complex terminology. They would prefer to have their public think that technical analysis is impossible without computers or a wealth of data. This view is incorrect. There are clear signs and symptoms of market tops and bottoms that are easily visible, readily recognized and available to anyone who is willing to take just a little time and effort to find them. They are based on the unmistakable lessons of market history, which I will cover in this book. Remember that these signs and symptoms are the product of reality-based information or, as noted earlier, market-generated information.

Regardless of the cycles and regardless of the technical or fundamental approach, several facts are relevant. They are:

- No market moves persistently higher without a corrective decline. This decline is inevitable.

- Sooner or later all bull markets and bear markets come to an end, as do all periods of economic growth and all periods of economic contraction.

- When tops come in economies and in stocks, there is often a confluence of events that contribute to the top.

- Traders and investors tend to focus on one or two major and obvious reasons for market and economic tops, often blaming them on major events. Y2K is a handy whipping boy for a pending market decline.

■ Many individual traders have made a large amount of money in the biggest bull market ever. Many have taken their profits. Typically this money will be reinvested when prices decline.

■ The easier it becomes to make money in a market, the closer the market is apt to be to its final peak.

■ Market declines are larger and faster than market rallies. Frequently rallies that took years to develop can have most of their gains erased in a fraction of the time it took for prices to reach their highs.

■ Stock markets are subject to boom-and-bust cycles as are virtually all markets and economic variables. The current cycle has been in a boom phase for an excessively long period of time.

■ Interest rates have played a key role in the direction of the U.S. stock market. Persistently declining rates have forced investors and money managers into stocks in order to maximize yields. When interest rates begin to move higher in earnest there will be a dramatic and potentially cataclysmic shift from stocks into higher yielding interest rate vehicles.

Where a great potential for profit exists, there is also a great potential for loss. Many investors who have done well in buying stocks are unfamiliar with the way in which markets can decline and eliminate profits with great speed. Hence, they are likely to be caught unaware by a sudden and "unexpected" decline.

A False Sense of Security

Given the persistence of this stock market boom and given the fact that market corrections have been fairly brief, many investors have been lulled into a false sense of security. Their view is that every decline is ultimately an opportunity to buy more stock. When the game ends, when stocks decline sharply and do not rally, those who own stocks and those who bought more stocks on the decline will be forced to liquidate. The ensuing panic liquidation will fuel a chain reaction of declines.

The timing of this top is a crucial consideration. Many traders fear it will come on the heels of bad news. I, however, feel that the top is more likely to develop following a wave of good news. Savvy investment professionals will use the good news to distribute holdings to an unsuspecting public. This, however, can only go so far since professionals control the vast majority of money in the market. Hence, if stocks sell off and the public's ability to buy has been depleted, this leaves only professionals to buy from other professionals. Since most professional traders (i.e., pension fund and mutual fund managers) view the market in generally similar fashion, there may be considerably more sellers than there are buyers.

Attempts to curb trading to prevent panic liquidation in the stock market may only add to investor anxiety. Finally, the impact of foreign stock markets on the U.S. stock market is a "wild card" variable since we have had only limited experience with chain-reaction buying and selling in foreign markets.

There is no magical power to the end of the millennium. I'm certain that my point of view will rub many a millennium fanatic the wrong way, but I am a realist, not a purveyor of psychic expectations. Even if there were any mystical power in the Year 2000, we have been given ample warning of what may occur and it therefore behooves us to prepare. Adequate and focused preparation will be our financial and personal salvation in the event of severe problems. If you have read books and articles about Y2K whose intent was to shock, then you will find this book distinctly different. My approach is slow, steady, relaxed and based on fact, not fiction; analysis, not hysteria.

This book is a warning as well as a guide to proactive preparedness. And the key will be timing as opposed to general expectations. It is my hope that the present discussion of signs and symptoms will assist you with timing. Should the actual timing of my expected market trend reversal coincide with the Year 2000, then so be it. Market timing is never exact. A host of variables enter into the decision-making process. Major economic events could occur either several months prior to or up to several years subsequent to the Year 2000. Regardless of what happens, the millennium mania groups will resound in a chorus of "we told you so."

Danger of the Self-Fulfilling Prophecy

Let's return to our analogy mentioned in the Introduction: You're in a crowded theater. The audience is transfixed as they watch the hero punish the villain. Someone notices a small flame under one of the seats. Apparently someone had been smoking illegally, dropped his lit cigarette on a potato chip bag, and the bag has caught fire. Instead of quietly stepping on the burning bag, or getting an usher, the person stands up and yells *FIRE* at the top of his voice. Instantly people are shrieking, pushing and shoving. Panic reigns as the crazed and fearful mob heads for the same exit. People are killed in the stampede. Meantime, the fire is quietly extinguished by a fast thinking and methodical usher who watches in disbelief as the panic grows. People stream out of the theater like rats leaving a sinking ship. The ship doesn't sink, and in spite of the fear, the theater doesn't burn, but people are nonetheless killed or maimed.

Note that I do not blame the new millennium directly for any situation that may occur. What could begin as a small burning potato chip bag in the theater of the stock market could easily mushroom into a serious forest fire. What may begin as a minor and fully manageable fire could, due to investor anxiety prompted by Year 2000 fears, develop into a serious panic with far-reaching implications.

Although the beginning of a new millennium will not necessarily be a cause in and of itself, it could well be perceived as a cause that in turn may trigger a chain reaction of catastrophic market events. Remember that *most market activity is based on expectations and perceptions.* If expectations and perceptions are distorted, then actions will be distorted. And distorted actions make for distorted market moves. It will be difficult to keep your wits about you if the dire Year 2000 forecasts continue. Here is yet another example of the warnings that persist:

> If we don't fix [the computers], there will be 90 million people 21 months from now who won't get refunds. The whole financial system of the United States will come to a halt.*

---

* Charles Rossotti, IRS Commissioner, *USA TODAY,* April 2, 1998.

Summary

Preparing for the millennium is something that can, and should, be done judiciously. It does not necessarily need to be a source of dread. Rather, it is something you need to consider and evaluate objectively. Assess the possible ramifications for you, your family and your business. Then prepare for what might happen by following a logical series of steps in a well-thought-out, methodical manner. Do not make any decisions based on hysteria. This book will be a valuable aid in helping you prepare and react without panic.

WHAT WILL HAPPEN IF THE MILLENNIUM BUG BITES?

American Zen philosopher Alan Watts observed that progress is often illusory. In his book, *The Taboo Against Knowing Who You Are,* Watts noted that scientific progress made by humankind tends to have an opposite effect. In other words, progress tends to bring on its own set of problems. With increased industrialization and production we have improved the overall standard of living for billions of people. Yet this progress has been at the cost of increased pollution as well as increased pressure to compete, which brings increased stress. Insecticides have allowed us to kill pests that reduce crop yields. However, they have also been linked to increased cancer rates resulting from toxins in the food we eat. Antibiotics have saved millions of lives, yet we are now at a point where resistant microbe strains have developed into diseases that threaten to kill millions. Deforestation of the Amazon has been lucrative for South American lumber producers; however, as a result, a variety of deadly microbes have been introduced into populated areas as their host carriers (jungle animals) come into contact with humans.

There will always be another reality to make fiction to the truth we think we've arrived at.

—Christopher Fry

Genetic engineering will soon allow us to produce human spare parts and to clone people as well as animals. This creates unprecedented moral, ethical and religious conflicts. Atomic energy promises vast power sources at minimal cost, yet it also brings with it the potential for mass human destruction. Advances in microbiology have allowed scientists to understand genetics and to cure diseases. These same advances have allowed demagogues to produce biological weapons of mass destruction. Who has the right to live as a result of medical progress? Is it the super rich or do the poor have as much right to the benefits of progress as the rich do? All progress tends to create other issues, some of which may, in fact, be more threatening than the problems that progress solved.

The Y2K situation is, perhaps, the most clearcut example of how the evolution of progress threatens to create *devolution.* We have, in the 1990s, come face to face with our growing dependence and reliance on technology. It is the progress of computer as machine and slave to humankind that now threatens to enslave its creator. In Andrew Lloyd Webber's *Phantom of the Opera,* Christine laments, "What I once dreamed I now dread." This could well be the mantra of computer owners the world over. While businesses and governments spend trillions to squash the Millennium Bug, programmers, software producers and hardware manufacturers will flourish as they are called upon to clean up the mess.

If you are at all interested in the Millennium Bug and the problems that may happen when the Year 2000 arrives, then I may be repeating what you already know. Yet the ramifications of Y2K problems are so vast, so all-encompassing, that it's difficult for the average person to get a clear grasp of what may happen and how it may all come about. It seems as if each discipline has its own set of expectations and warnings. Y2K experts can be found everywhere. Opinions as to what may come in Y2K are many and varied. If you've spent any time "surfing" the many Y2K Internet web sites, you know exactly what I'm talking about. Given this extreme diversity of opinion, I think it's pertinent to examine the situation carefully.

Here is an overview of what may happen when the Millennium Bug finally makes its presence known. I will attempt to cover the relevant major categories. Since no one knows for sure what will happen, and there are radical views in every sector, in the end you must decide for yourself. To do that, you need to know what to expect.

Essence of the Problem

The Y2K bug issue is based on a simple but understandable blunder. Back in the 1960s and 1970s when computer technology was in its relative infancy, the cost of memory and storage devices (i.e., tape and disk drives) were at a premium. I bought my first computer in the 1970s. It was a Data General Nova 3/12 System. It boasted 32K of memory and a massive 10-megabyte hard drive. The system was the size of two side-by-side refrigerators and the removable hard disk was about 16 inches in diameter. The system cost me about $30,000 as I recall (and that was $30,000 in 1970s' dollars!). Today a system with 64 MB of memory and a 6-gigabyte drive can be had for about $1500. Yes, things have changed.

Yet in the 1970s when systems were expensive, storage was limited and memory was miniscule by today's standards, it was necessary to conserve as much space as possible on the disk drives and to process information in memory as efficiently as possible. The obvious and seemingly ingenious solution was to drop the first two digits of each year's date. Hence, 1977 would appear as 77. While two digits doesn't seem like much, in the long run, over billions of repetitions, it adds up to an incredible amount of space. Programmers understandably made the decision to "deal" with the issue at a later date when memory and storage were bound to be much cheaper.

Time and technology have progressed, but the seriousness of the issue was not recognized or dealt with early enough to ensure a smooth transition. What do I mean by a smooth transition and why is a transition necessary? The answer is simple. Because there are literally trillions of entries (or more) in computers all over the world that are date related, these two-digit year codes must be altered. In the process of making the change, it is necessary to safeguard the integrity of systems that are currently working as well as those that will now be required to read dates in the new millennium.

This is not an easy task since many dates are embedded in files where they may not be easily found. Furthermore, the original programs must be able to work with the new dates, or the new programs must be able to read the old dates without confusing the two-digit codes. It's not only a programming nightmare, but it also has hardware implications. The so-called "bios chip" in many computers is designed to read only the two-number year code. Therefore, when the year 2000 begins, the computer with an old chip will read 00 as 1900 and not 2000. This could cause a whole chain reaction of program failures. If you use scheduling software, you could miss appointments and birthdays, but the real danger is that programs will fail and records may not be accessible.

The potential problems are staggering. Consider the following scenarios:

THE *!#$@!#!! MONEY MACHINE WON'T COOPERATE

You go to your ATM to withdraw money on Jan. 2, 2000. Your card is rejected since the machine can't read the 00. You're frustrated. Just a few days ago (still in 1999) the darned thing worked. Why doesn't it work now? You thought your bank was ready for Y2K. Well, guess what; your bank thought it was ready, too. Millions of bank and credit card customers feel secure in the fact that when their new credit cards arrived they showed a year 01 expiration date. This led them (and you) to believe that all was well in the land of bits, bytes and Y2K. Clearly this was wrong. The mere printing of a credit card or ATM access card doesn't make the Y2K problems go away.

The simple fact of the matter is that although your card was read by the system, the system had no idea what your card meant. Just because the expiration date on the card showed as 01, it doesn't mean for a moment that the computer knew what it was looking at on that day in January. Anyone can manufacture a credit card, but not all computers will be able to read the card correctly after the year turns to 00. This little inconvenience is only the tip of the iceberg. Within the whirring core of the bank computer resides a massive amount of computer code both in "written" form and in "hard wired" form (i.e., circuitry). And it must all be changed in order to accommodate the Year 2000 dates.

THE NEW YEAR'S EVE PARTY

You're attending a fantastic Millennium New Year's Eve party on December 31, 1999. What an outstanding event! Ringing in a new millennium is truly a once-in-a-lifetime opportunity. As midnight approaches the roar of the crowd intensifies. Many New Year's Eve celebrations have come before but this one is particularly intense since there are so many uncertainties as the millennium ends and the year 2000 approaches. The final 60 seconds of the countdown begin. All eyes are on the clock. Anticipation builds. The mixture of tension and frivolity is difficult to define but its presence is unmistakable. Will the new millennium begin with a bang or a whimper? Will computers the world over fail or will the new millennium come in quietly? Midnight comes and goes without incident. The crowd breathes a sigh of relief. The lights are still on, televisions and radios are working, traffic lights outside are functioning well and there are no unexpected air raid sirens.

The party begins to break up at 1 a.m. A few people have already left and wait patiently by the elevators eager to beat the drunks back home. Your wait at the elevator seems unbearably long; however, there are 500 people at the party so a delay is not unreasonable. After 15 minutes, a fairly large crowd has formed. You're becoming concerned but the idea of walking down 60 flights of stairs isn't your idea of a good way to begin the new millennium. So you wait. And you wait. The crowd has now grown to several hundred strong. Some have decided to take the stairs, but others are still inebriated and don't realize what's happening.

The growing throng of party-goers has no idea that the elevators are stuck between floors. Trapped in the elevator are five unfortunate souls who were unable to stay at the party until the stroke of midnight. They entered the elevator at several minutes before midnight, only to have it stop dead in its tracks between the 27th and 28th floors. When it stopped and the emergency lights went on, there was a reasonable amount of concern; however, panic was avoided when one of the occupants noted that there were "hundreds of people in the building who will hear the alarm." But the revelers were noisy and the alarm went unheard. To make matters worse, the emergency telephone in the elevator was dead.

Why did the elevators stop? The computer-controlled building security system turned off the elevators at the stroke of midnight when, failing to understand the meaning of 01/01/00 on its internal clock, it assumed (as programmed) that burglars were attempting to circumvent its security codes. The elevators were programmed to stop between floors in the event of a building break-in, thus preventing burglars from using the elevators to cart off stolen goods. Although the manufacturer of the security system claimed it was Y2K ready, their tests did not detect problems embedded within their computer code.

THE TRAFFIC CONTROL NIGHTMARE

11:47 P.M. December 31, 1999. Air Traffic Control Center: Joliet, Illinois —Two veteran air traffic controllers sit at their large radar tracking screens in the dimly lit tower. The amber screens show light traffic tonight as the millennium approaches. In quiet conversation the two controllers discuss their displeasure at having to work this night. They exchange a few jokes about the Y2K madness that has been sweeping the world. Having been through at least a dozen tests of their air traffic control system over the last few months, they're confident of its Y2K readiness. The screens show 14 flights on their final approach to Chicago's O'Hare International Airport, with 18 outbound flights en route to other locations. The weather is ideal. Midnight comes. The controllers shake hands, wishing each other a healthy and prosperous year 2000. Glancing back at his screen one of the controllers is gripped by sudden panic. Three blips have disappeared from his screen. Looking over at his fellow controller he realizes that she, too, has "lost" a few flights. Where are they? What could have happened to them? The FAA has certified all of its operations and computers 98 percent Y2K ready. How could a "lil ole 2 percent" cause this?

Although the FAA did its job as well as could be expected, the sad fact is that some of the airlines failed to do their Y2K compliance thoroughly. The cost of correcting potential Y2K problems in onboard transponders and communications systems was simply too large a drain on their finances. So they cut some corners, "streamlined" some operations and estimated that most of their planes would be Y2K ready. As an added protection they grounded planes whose Y2K readiness was questionable.

Why did the identification blips disappear? Apparently the transponders that send out tracking signals to air traffic radar failed to operate due to invalid date codes generated by their "burned in" chips. The manufacturer assured airlines that these units would be Y2K ready when retrofitted with new chips. They were wrong. For reasons that may take several months to determine, the transponders stopped working. As improbable and as impossible as this turn of events seemed to be, it was happening, and all the controllers could do was to track these flights using voice communications and other manual guidance systems until they were safely brought to a landing. The only fear now was that these systems would fail, too.

While I could give many more examples, I'm certain you realize that the problems, come Y2K, could be global and severe. In an article entitled *More than Just Computers Vulnerable to Y2K,** M. J. Zuckerman points out that a shortage of expertise has resulted in U.S. Y2K firms farming out their work to programmers in India, Pakistan, Ireland and the Philippines. To give you an idea of what work still has to be done, the author notes that Provident Bank of Cincinnati requires 8.5 million lines of computer code to upgrade their systems to Y2K readiness. And this is only one bank!

Overview of Problems and Fixes

As you can see, the implications are vast. What follows is a general overview of potential problem areas.

COMPUTERS

Home, business and government computers are all vulnerable to the Y2K date problem. Although computer chips may have been upgraded, there may still be problems with operating systems, particularly old versions of Windows, DOS and commercial operating systems. They could completely shut down. The simple fix is to upgrade the operating system. However, in some cases, the available memory or disk space won't accommodate the new operating system software, and some older computers won't accommodate memory upgrades beyond a certain maximum. In many cases computers will need to be entirely scrapped. If this is the case, then you are advised to do so promptly. Waiting will not change the situation.

---

* Zuckerman, M. J., *Chicago Tribune,* November 13, 1998.

Even if you are successful in upgrading your hardware to Y2K readiness, your programs may not be Y2K ready. Hence, old versions of programs like Microsoft Word, Excel or PageMaker may not work. You may need to upgrade all programs. Finally, you will also need to check your peripheral devices such as modems and printers to make certain they are Y2K ready. As you can see, the process could well be an involved, costly and complicated one. In most cases it will be more efficient and cost effective to scrap the systems and begin with new ones. However, it must be noted that if you have an old database, this data will need to be converted to Y2K compatibility or it will not work on your new system. Again, the problems are many, varied and costly.

While the costs and problems for home computers are not overwhelming, they are significant for business and government. Initial cost estimates were severely understated. I believe that Y2K will be more costly on an international level than any problem ever encountered. On the one hand it will be a windfall for those in the Y2K business; on the other, it will deal a serious blow to operating profits and to the budgets of government agencies. Since a vast amount of the money being spent in upgrading computer code will go to programmers outside the U.S., the impact on our economy could be substantial.

COMPUTER CHIPS IN OTHER SYSTEMS

As you know, computers and computerized controls are everywhere. They are involved in every phase of our lives from manufacturing to traffic lights, from your microwave oven to your automobile's suspension system control. There is no getting away from the fact that we have become dependent on computers. The painful realization of this dependency if there is a Y2K crisis will be a great lesson to us. It will be as much of a shocker as was the launch of *Sputnik I,* the U.S. atomic bomb drops on Japan and the AIDS threat. We will learn that we are not invincible. Creature comforts we now have are dependent on computer chips and computer controls. Although most of these will not fail because they are not date dependent, some will cause problems.

The most serious potential problems for your home are breakdowns in home security systems, telephone communications and home heating/cooling controls. These could result in major breakdowns and must be taken care of immediately. Such problems will be especially serious in businesses whose security systems may fail. What's worse is that such systems use telephone lines to alert the security monitoring company. In the event that these systems fail, the result may very well prove to be a bonanza for burglars and looters. Should this occur, you can expect considerable unrest as well as a calling up of the National Guard or worse.

There has been much said about the potential for civil unrest and rioting. While I do not anticipate it, it is certainly a possibility not only in the United States but in other parts of the world as well. I believe that the severity of such a situation depends a great deal on the preparedness of governments. Should such things as Social Security checks, welfare checks and food stamps be unavailable, the consequences may be severe. Anger and frustration could result, and there is no telling how things will play out.

I anticipate most other problems as they relate to home computers will be less serious, resulting in smaller inconveniences. The serious problems will arise in industry, manufacturing, broadcasting and government control systems. The effects of these problems could have a significant ripple-down impact on world economies unless actions are taken to correct them.

To a great extent, other problems that may develop as a result of outdated computer chips in a variety of uses is intangible. While isolated problems may occur, I suspect that if they are dealt with promptly, there will be no serious consequences. The real danger, however, is the possibility that a chain reaction of malfunctions will occur. This is why I stress the importance of being prepared both personally (i.e., in your home and with your finances) and in your business.

COMMUNICATIONS

We have also become dependent on electronic communications. Whether these are in the form of radio, television, Internet, satellite, ISDN line, telephone, cellular phone or otherwise, they are all now inextricably intertwined with computers. Computers are at the heart of all modern communications. Perhaps the only forms of electronic communication not under direct computer control in one sense or another are walkie-talkies, amateur radio or CB radio. A breakdown in communications poses a serious threat to all world economies, to all businesses, to electronic commerce, to personal finance and to your health.

Many people fail to realize that virtually all commerce is now transacted electronically. This holds true in bank fund transfers, brokerage accounts, stocks and commodity transactions, medicine and more. That is why I believe this is the single largest problem area. All you need to do is use your imagination and you will see what can happen. A simple way to examine this situation is to take nothing in your daily life for granted if it is in any way related to technology. It's that simple and it's that scary!

Much has been said about banking problems, problems in transacting security and commodity business and problems on the trading floors of exchanges throughout the world. I lump all of these into the area of communications since it is a breakdown in communications that may cause such problems.

Given the scope and extent of potential problems in this area, the solutions must be definitive. The danger of a chain reaction in finance and industry as a result of inefficient, nonfunctional or erroneous communications is the most threatening aspect of the Y2K problem. This is the area that concerns most forecasters and analysts, and it is the area for which you must be as completely prepared as possible. Since there are so many aspects to the general area of communications, it is essential that you investigate your own preparedness and institute proper corrective measures.

FOOD, WATER, ESSENTIAL SERVICES

Most of our food and bottled water come to us by rail and then by truck to supermarkets. Truck and train deliveries are often scheduled by computer. The possibility of computer problems disrupting such schedules is considerable. These computer problems may also affect food manufacturing, particularly in the case of processed foods that may depend on strict amounts of cooking or freezing time. While these problems may seem relatively simple to solve, they may not be so straightforward as you may think. You may want to find a farmer's market close to you in the event that fresh fruit and vegetable supplies are disrupted.

In this area I also include trash collection, electricity and water. There are widely varying degrees of Y2K preparedness in these areas. In some cases you can fully expect the power to go off and perhaps even the water supply. I urge you to do some investigating to find out if your city or town is fully prepared. You may also want to check with your local power company.

Waste disposal may also be affected. Schedules for such services are often maintained via computer and the Y2K bug could adversely affect these. Don't be surprised to see garbage piling up in major cities all over the world. Paradoxically, I suspect that those nations that are least dependent on computers will have the fewest problems in these areas.

MEDICAL

Here is another major area of concern. Medicine is more computerized today than ever before. Diagnostic tests are evaluated by computer, patient files and records are stored on computers drug manufacturers are heavily dependent on computers, and reporting of patient lab results is often done via computer or FAX machine. There is the distinct danger of a breakdown in medical services as a result of Y2K problems. My greatest concern here is the possible threat to human life for patients in critical care or who are dependent on medications that may not be available in the event of manufacturing or supply disruptions. It is imperative that the medical community, including doctors, drug manufacturers, hospitals, nursing organizations, laboratories and insurance companies, be totally prepared for Y2K problems. You are individually best prepared by determining in advance your medical needs and the preparedness of your medical care providers.

NATIONAL SECURITY

There are concerns that international terrorist groups may attempt to take advantage of Y2K problems to launch attacks on their enemies. Yes, this is a real problem. Recently, CIA Director George Tenet stated before the Senate Special Committee on Y2K that "Y2K redemption provides opportunities for someone with hostile intent to understand how your computer works, how your business works and what your vulnerabilities are..." This is a cause for concern since (as stated earlier) a good deal of the Y2K code revisions are being done in foreign countries, some of which are not on the best of terms with the United States.

Furthermore, the possibility of weapons systems going haywire is perhaps the biggest threat. Rest assured that most countries consider this their highest priority and are diligently working to correct the problem. However, in countries that have weapons of mass destruction but limited resources to resolve potential Y2K problems, the situation is serious. Many experts are concerned about the possible erroneous or unintentional launch of a missile or air attack. Finally, consider the fact that exiled Saudi terrorist Osama bin Ladin is computer savvy and has a base of operations in the Philippines. A considerable amount of Y2K programming is being done in that country. Yes, it's food for thought and although it may be a large jump from the possible to the actual, it's something to be concerned about.

INFRASTRUCTURE

Although most municipalities in the United States are Y2K ready or close to ready, there are some cities that do not have the resources to adequately prepare. In such cases there could be problems with municipal water supplies, electricity, traffic control systems, police, fire, 911 emergency and emergency medical systems. While these are not matters of national security, they could make life in town difficult for a few days or longer. Various cities throughout the world may not be so ready as are U.S. municipalities. You will need to look into your local situation to get the answers.

Summary

These are the major areas of concern. I am not an alarmist; however, I do believe that knowledge of what could happen is the first step to preparation. Admittedly some of these things are not within your control. We will have to hope that those who are responsible in government and industry are doing their jobs. However, you bear full responsibility for your personal and business preparedness. Do what is necessary, but do it logically, methodically and, above all, *don't panic!*

INTEREST RATES:
KEY TO MARKET DIRECTION

It has become virtually axiomatic, particularly in the 1980s and 1990s, that the direction of many world stock markets is intricately

> ... when the world financial crisis began so unexpectedly with the October 1929 market crash, nothing turned out as expected . . .*
>
> —Donald D. Hoppe

related to the direction and level of interest rates. The low cost of money is fuel for economic progress in a capitalist society. Generally speaking, the higher the cost of money, the lower the probability of business expansion and borrowing. But the cost of money is a two-edged sword. In modern capitalist societies, governments manipulate the cost of money in terms of how they evaluate the current state of economic affairs.

When the Economy Is Growing "Backwards"

When economic conditions are slow and business is not growing at a reasonable pace, or when economic growth is at a relative standstill, governments will lower interest rates in order to stimulate borrowing

---

* Hoppe, Donald D., *The Kondratieff Wave Analyst*, 11(8), August 1987.

and, as a result, spending. This is what was happening in Japan from 1990–1998. Due to the very poor state of the Japanese economy, the government has persistently lowered interest rates in an effort to stimulate the economy.

In late 1990 the long-term Japanese government bond yield was at about 8.2 percent. Since then it has declined persistently to about 1.5 percent, the lowest rate in many years. The effort here is twofold. One goal is to discourage savings (money being placed in banks) and to encourage investing (money in stocks and businesses) where the return is likely to be higher. The second goal is to encourage spending on large items such as automobiles and homes. The hope is that the investor will find such buying attractive due to the low cost of borrowing money. Yet, neither of these two objectives has been achieved in Japan as the economy has continued its decline.

If rates are lowered and new borrowing or consumer demand is not detected, they will be lowered repeatedly, often in small increments until there is an increase in borrowing both by businesses and consumers. As I stated above, this has not happened. By contrast, this has indeed been the case, at least partially, in the United States and Europe. Figures 3.1 and 3.2 show the relationship between the U.S. stock market and interest rate yields. As you can see, there has been a generally inverse relationship. As interest rates have declined, the stock market has rallied. But let's examine these relationships in greater detail.

Referring to Figure 3.1 please note the following:

- From about early 1940 through about 1946, interest rates were declining. This period of declining interest rates was accompanied by an upward trend in stock prices.

- From about 1960 through about 1967, interest rates moved lower as stocks moved higher.

- As interest rates moved strongly higher from 1966 through 1975, it was difficult for stock prices to maintain a sustained move to higher levels.

- From 1983 until 1998, the decline in interest rates has been relatively persistent and relatively large. It is during this same period of time that the U.S. stock market has had its longest and most sustained up-market in history.

Granted, this view is simplistic, and there have been periods of time that did not conform to this general pattern, but this is merely a first

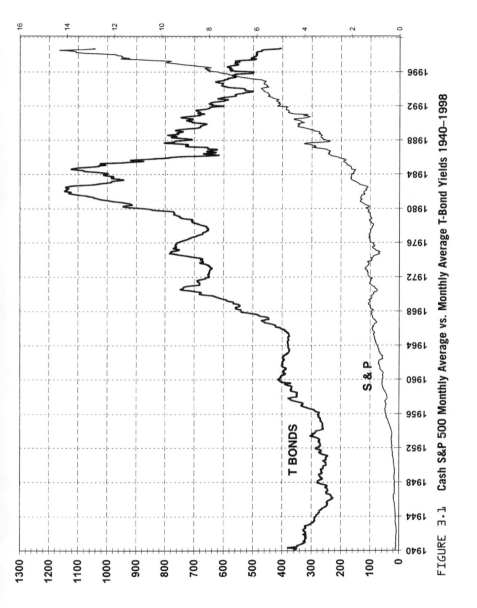

FIGURE 3.1 Cash S&P 500 Monthly Average vs. Monthly Average T-Bond Yields 1940–1998

33

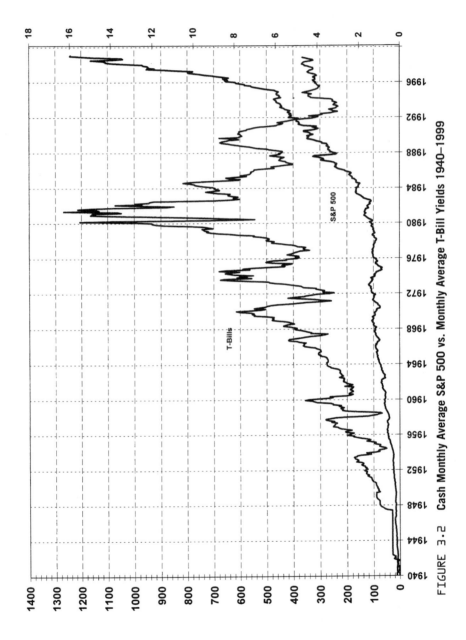

FIGURE 3.2 Cash Monthly Average S&P 500 vs. Monthly Average T-Bill Yields 1940–1999

34

stop in examining a series of patterns that will help us understand the stock market and the economy as a whole. Interest rates are a key factor in the engine that drives economies worldwide. The U.S. government through its Federal Reserve System is a major force behind stock prices, stock market trends and the economy by virtue of their control over interest rates.

Capitalist governments the world over actively control interest rates by expanding and contracting the supply of money in order to influence and adjust the rate of economic growth. At times their efforts are effective and well planned, but at times their actions are politically inspired, self-serving and subject to the manipulation of groups with a vested interest. We cannot, therefore, assume that the actions of governments are always instituted with the best interest of the general public in mind.*

When the Economy Is Growing "Too Fast"

When business is strong and an economy is growing too fast, governments are concerned that too much money may be chasing too few goods. In other words, they fear inflation and decide to apply the brakes. They raise interest rates repeatedly until there are indications that expansion is slowing and that consumer demand has cooled off. Higher rates will, slowly but surely, dissuade borrowing both by consumers and businesses, thereby slowing economic expansion and, at least theoretically, decreasing the possibility of inflation. There is, in theory, no limit to how high interest rates need to be raised in order to slow the engines of economic growth. The idea is clearly that too much growth is just as dangerous as too little growth.

When the United States economy was growing too rapidly and stock prices were accelerating during the 1970s, the government repeatedly raised interest rates until consumer demand dropped and prices declined across a broad front. One of the most telltale signs of

---

* I strongly recommend William Greider's *Secrets of the Temple: How the Federal Reserve Runs the Country* (New York: Touchstone Books, 1989). This revealing book explains how the Federal Reserve, essentially accountable to no one, has immense power to control the nation's economy and its markets. The potential dangers of such vast power to influence trends should be a source of concern to all investors.

explosive inflation was the price of gold and silver. Both markets tend to rise during periods of excessive growth and contract during periods when growth is slow. Figure 3.3 shows the monthly price of cash gold versus T-bond yields in the late 1970s when the last inflationary peak was reached. Interest rates were raised repeatedly until the fires of inflation were calmed and gold prices declined.

As you can see, there is a relationship not only between interest rates and the stock market but also between gold prices (in fact, between virtually all commodity prices) and interest rates. While the relationship is not one to one, it is generally valid and can be used quite effectively to gauge periods of economic inflation and deflation.

The Flight to "Quality"

Still another aspect of interest rate relationships is the so-called "flight to quality." This can occur during a time of economic crisis and may well be an important relationship to remember during any Y2K crisis that may surface during late 1999 or in the first few years of the new millennium. The importance of what I am about to tell you extends beyond any millennium crisis. During times of economic crisis, in particular during a banking or currency crisis, large investors and traders liquidate holdings in stocks and place their cash into what they consider to be safe havens for temporary keeping. Such safe havens are usually Treasury bonds and/or Treasury bills. Although the interest rate yield on these vehicles may be very small, they are considered safer than other vehicles during times of crisis since they are issued by the U.S. government and, to a given extent, backed by the government. In such cases investors have opted to sacrifice higher yields for safety.

If you are concerned about the safety of your money in a bank, you are advised to take those funds, well in advance of any crisis, and place them into U.S. government Treasury bonds and/or Treasury bills. While you won't get much return on your money, you will benefit from the relative safety of these vehicles.

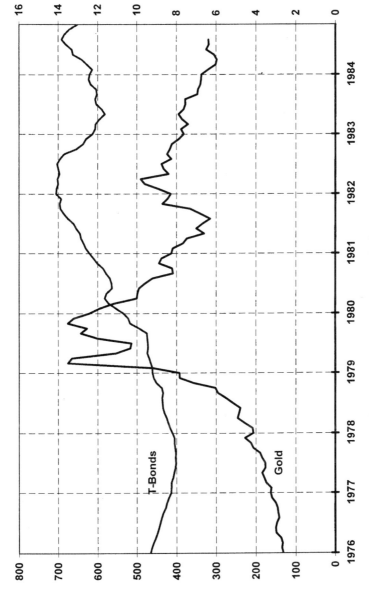

FIGURE 3.3   Monthly Average Price of Cash Gold vs. Monthly Average T-Bond Yields in the Late 1970s through mid 1980s

Interest Rates in the New Millennium

As you can see from the charts I've presented, interest rates are at their lowest level in many years. This very low level created an environment that has contributed to the major upward move of the stock market since the early 1980s. What follows is a description of the conditions that led to this big stock market rally, and some things to consider come the new millennium. Note that all of these conditions will likely play an important role in whatever happens. Remember that the cost of money is what drives the economy as well as the stock market.

IMPACT OF LOW INTEREST RATES ON STOCK PRICES

Because investors have not been able to get much of a return on their money by keeping it in banks, they have been forced to put their money into vehicles that will give them a higher return. Typically this means they will put their money into stocks that provide a higher return (i.e., dividends) than compound interest in a savings account. In addition to the low rates on savings accounts and Treasury bonds, commercial paper yields have also been low. As a result, the average investor has been "punished" for keeping money in the bank. Even with the relatively low rate of inflation, the money earned from savings has been insufficient to attract any savvy investor.

The declining level of interest rates on savings has also put pressure on professional money managers who are "under the gun" to produce profits for their clients. They have been forced to buy stocks in order to show their clients growth on their investments.

The combination of relatively low inflation, a government that has exercised reasonable fiscal responsibility, good consumer demand bolstered by high employment and relatively stable commodity prices have all fostered the growth of the stock market. Money managers have seen corporate earnings grow, which justifies their heavy investment in stocks.

As stocks have increased in price and as earnings in most sectors have grown, investors have been rewarded handsomely for their actions. There has never been a more stable or more rewarding stock market that has persisted for so many years, and the ability of stocks to bounce back strongly following every major decline since the 1980s has been even more impressive to investors and money managers.

Billions of investor dollars have flowed into mutual funds. Accordingly, fund managers have had no choice but to put that money into stocks. This has added fuel to an already overheated market. With demand for stocks as strong as it has been, professional money managers have searched high and low to find investments that might give them a reasonable return on their money. This has caused the price of virtually all stocks that have growth potential and reasonable dividends to be pushed to higher and higher levels.

Finally, as is the case in all major bull markets, speculators have bet not only on current earnings but also on future earnings. In some cases, stocks with virtually no earnings or even less than no earnings have been bought aggressively in the anticipation of growth. The speculative frenzy feeds on itself as prices soar. This has been particularly true of Internet-related stocks. Prices have been bid up to absurd levels that make some of the speculative manias of the past look tame by comparison.

And so the stage is set for a potentially significant change in trend and in market psychology. Later, I will discuss the history and role of excessive speculation, relating it to the recent and current market environment. I will also show you how economic patterns, especially price patterns and interest rates, are now combining to create a confluence of major events which may cause a major economic catastrophe. As you read on, remember one thing above all: The lessons you will learn in this book about patterns and relationships will help you no matter what the underlying economic environment may be.

Hundreds of "What-Ifs"

There are hundreds of *what-ifs* as we approach the Year 2000 and beyond. Here are some of the questions that have been raised by professional market analysts as well as individual investors.

- What if my brokerage firm can't process my orders and I can't buy or sell stocks?
- What if I can't get cash out of my brokerage account?
- What if the stock and commodity exchanges can't process orders because of computer problems?
- How will I be able to trade electronically via the Internet if communications go down as a result of Y2K problems?

- What if my telephone doesn't work due to Y2K problems?
- What if computers on the exchange floor cannot keep track of transactions and the prices I get on my quotation machine are incorrect or delayed?
- What if my quotation machine doesn't work and I can't get stock or commodity price quotes?
- What if I can't liquidate positions in my mutual fund holdings?
- What if I buy a stock and can't get out because my broker's phone lines fail?
- What if the price quotations I get are incorrect and I don't know it?

All of the above are valid questions and concerns. The simple answer to all of them is to be prudent and to approach each situation cautiously at first. I will give you more specific guidelines about how to proceed under conditions that may prevail from mid- to late 1999 until well into the year 2002. It is during this time frame that problems, if any, are likely to surface. By the time you read this, some problems may already have started to develop.

In order to understand what may happen in the financial markets, let's take a look at the big picture and see how interest rates, the stock market, panics and price patterns relate to one another. I am a firm believer in the fact that major events in history and in the markets occur when numerous patterns come together at about the same time. Such "confluence" is important and will prove to be significant during the next few years. Above and beyond what happens during the period of a possible millennium crisis, the patterns we are discussing are likely to be valid for many years to come. They are based on history and can, therefore, assist you in all types of economic environments regardless of whether they occur at or near the start of the Year 2000.

Crashes, Panics, Pundits and Prophecies

Panics, crashes and prognostications are not new to the markets. As long as markets have existed, there have been prophecies of gloom and doom. As long as there will be markets there will be prognosticators. Forecasts will be based on everything from Bible verses to Tarot cards. Astrologers will find planetary configurations that portend crashes and panics. Psychics will apply their "skills" to forecasting dire economic events and crashes in the stock market. As the millennium draws to an end there will be more forecasts from all types of forecasters; many will seem somewhat credible. After all, we live in a world dependent on computers and computer technology. Without computers, things just won't work. And if it's true, as many would have us believe, that virtually every area of life that depends on computers will come to a standstill on January 1, 2000, then the seemingly incredible forecasts become credible. The best we can do as rational and thinking human beings is to sit back and evaluate the facts. Although we're not blessed with the Vulcan intelligence and logic of *Star Trek*'s Mr. Spock, we do have at our disposal a plethora of facts as well as the lessons of history. If we don't learn from the lessons of history, then we are destined to repeat the mistakes.

Forecasts: Blessing or Curse?

Many traders believe in the value and power of forecasts; they follow them religiously. I believe that a forecast without specific timing is essentially useless unless you have the patience of a saint. There are stock market forecasters who, for many years, have been predicting a collapse in the U.S. market. They have been wrong year after year. One such forecaster (without mentioning a name) has become what is called in the philosophy of logic a "reliable anti-authority." Virtually every time he has uttered a forecast of doom and gloom for the U.S. stock market and/or economy, reality has come back to bite him hard. Still he has persisted.

Sex Appeal and Stocks

For over a decade, as stock markets the world over have been rallying to all-time highs, this forecaster has continued to preach an end to the big bull market. And still the march continues to higher levels, as if to spite him. He is not alone. He has good company. There are literally hundreds of gloom and doomers out there just waiting to find problems. Forecasts are sexy; however, without timing a forecast can serve no constructive purpose. (This, by the way, holds true for my forecasts as well. As you may know, when I publish my forecasts I try to provide timing ideas that will confirm or negate my expectations. While I am not always successful in doing so, I have reminded my clients and readers repeatedly that my work *must be confirmed* by timing.)

A "Wall of Worry"

Controversial, colorful, irreverent, but always entertaining market timer, Joe Granville, often described the stock market as climbing a "wall of worry." There are many analysts and prognosticators who hang their hats on virtually every possible piece of negative news. If it's not a crisis in Russia, then it's a crisis in the Federal Reserve System. And if it's not a crisis in the personal life of a U.S. president, then it must be a financial crisis in Asia that will undo the U.S. economy. Yes, sooner or later they'll be right, but sooner or later, if we're wrong too many times, we run out of money and can't play the game. Markets tend to climb a wall of worry. They often rally on bad news—and on good news—when the trend is bullish. And they often decline on good news—and on bad news—when the trend is bearish.

Trend and Timing—The Dynamic Duo

Trend is much more important than news, and timing is the companion of trend. Together, trend and timing are better than any forecast by any prognosticator. The only thing that may be better than trend and timing is inside information, and few of us are privy to truly useful inside information. (Note also that there are laws against the use of inside information.) So what's left? Trend and timing will survive when all else fails.

So what's wrong with a forecast? I'll tell you plain and simple: The danger in a forecast is that you may believe it. Yes, that's right—you may believe it. Then, you ask, what good is a forecast if it's not cogent and credible? The fact is that all the great forecasts of all the great forecasters are always humbled by the reality of economic life. To be worthwhile, a forecast must answer these questions:

- What is likely to happen?
- When is it likely to happen?

- How will we know if our expectations are to become realities?
- How much should we risk?
- How much should we expect to profit?
- When should we get out?
- How will we know if we are wrong?
- When will we know if we are wrong?

HUBRIS

Of the questions above, the two most important are *when* will we know if we are wrong and *what* will confirm that we are likely to be right. What is sorely lacking in most forecasts is this aspect of timing. Remember this when you read a forecast. Whether it's my forecast, something you hear from a friend, a taxi driver or a high-ranking government official, be careful! A Department of Energy official was quoted recently as stating that world supplies of crude oil are now so plentiful that there is unlikely to be any substantial or lasting increase in prices until well into the next millennium!

Is that a forecast or is it hubris? Without timing the forecast is essentially meaningless, although it does make for good press. After reading this book you should have the basic tools necessary to develop forecasts that include the approximate timing that will make them useful. Before we can get to this place we need to examine a few important patterns and historical examples, since they are highly important in determining what is likely to occur in the next millennium.

Interest Rates and the Stock Market Panic of 1929

As you know, the United States stock market soared from 1924 to 1929. Stock market speculation ran rampant in 1928 and 1929. As Figure 3.4 shows, the stock market average went from about 100 in 1924 to about 375 in 1929. The stock market of the 1920s was a wildly speculative market that soared on borrowed money. Realizing that the potential for a collapse in prices was very possible, the U.S. Treasury raised interest rates substantially. This was done in order to curb speculation. They reasoned that if money were more costly to

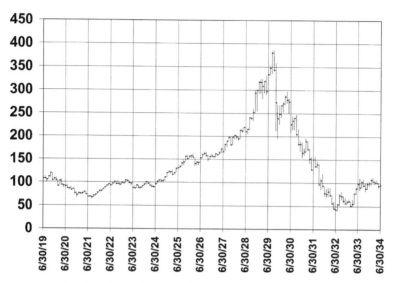

FIGURE 3.4   **Dow Jones Stock Market Average from 1919 to 1934**

borrow, then speculators would not be so willing to borrow in order to speculate. During the period from about late 1924 to about mid-1929, short-term interest rates as measured by Treasury bills rose from under 3 percent to about 9 percent. Figure 3.5 shows the rise in interest rates during this time.

The tripling of short-term interest rates ultimately had the desired effect. Following such a serious increase in the cost of short-term money, speculators became concerned that the stock market bubble would not last. In late October 1929 stocks fell sharply as traders sold stocks *en masse* fearing that the big bull market was over. The selling accelerated as investors panicked. The market declined on a broad front. Selling led to more selling as the avalanche continued.

The lessons of history are quite clear. In retrospect we know that the ability of investors and speculators to borrow 90 percent of the money they needed to buy stocks fueled the great bull market of the 1920s. We know that the market rally was built on a house of cards. The "Crash of 1929" or the "Panic Liquidation of 1929" as I prefer to call it, has been studied, analyzed, dissected, debated, discussed and reviewed by hundreds if not thousands of scholars and economists.

Historians have their view of the causes and effects of the panic, while economists and sociologists have theirs. There is likely some

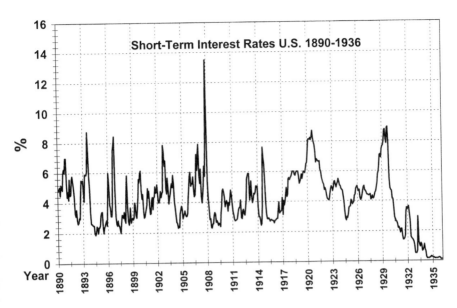

FIGURE 3.5   Interest Rates from 1890 to 1936

truth in every interpretation; however, in the final analysis several points about the Panic of 1929 are clear and indisputable:

- The stock market decline was, at first, a corrective move in response to high stock prices and excessive speculation.

- The stock market rise was a result of extremely low interest rates.

- The stock market rise was accentuated by low margin. Investors and speculators could buy stocks for 10 percent of their actual value, borrowing the additional 90 percent. Hence, a simplistic point of view might be that 90 percent of stock values were inflated, or conversely, that those stocks were only worth about 10 percent of the prices at which they were trading.

- In order to curb excessive speculation that resulted from the earlier low interest rates and low margin, the regulatory powers quickly raised interest rates until the cost of money made it unattractive to borrow for the purpose of speculation.

- Panic was instrumental in accelerating and exacerbating the decline. Had investors not panicked to the degree that they did, the market might not have fallen so fast or so far. This conclusion, of course, is open to debate and conjecture since we will never know if panic was instrumental in causing a worse decline than might otherwise have occurred.

- In retrospect, it appears that the rise in interest rates was too rapid and that it ultimately resulted in an unexpected, sudden and excessive decline during which stocks lost much of their value.

- The wave of bankruptcies that followed the Panic Liquidation of 1929 reverberated through the U.S. economy, causing a chain reaction of selling that eventually exerted a profound impact on every sector of the U.S. economy. To say that the Panic Liquidation of 1929 caused the Great Depression would be an overstatement of the facts; however, it was without a doubt a factor that exacerbated a situation that had been developing for quite some time.

- Finally, the Panic Liquidation of 1929 can be seen as a clear example of how a sharp and sudden rise in interest rates following a period of relative dormancy and low interest rates can have a marked and severe effect on stock prices and the U.S. economy in general.

- The lessons of this significant historical example have been heeded by governments the world over. Accordingly, when interest rates are raised in order to slow excessive growth, they are raised slowly, often just one-quarter percent at a time. Also, the margin requirement for buying stocks is kept at a reasonable level to limit excessive speculation and inflated stock prices.

- The 1929 example illustrated the significant role that interest rates and panic selling by speculators play in the control of economic growth and in the "regulation" of stock market trends and prices. The 1929 experience also sends a powerful message about panic. Those who panicked first to buy and then to sell suffered a double jeopardy. First, they bought stocks at or near the high and then they liquidated them as the market plunged. In addition to the key role that interest rates played in precipitating the Crash of 1929, there were many other factors and forces that preceded both the large speculative rally and the severe decline.

ASSIGNING BLAME

It is not uncommon for humans to assign blame. When we are wrong about something or when we have failed, we tend to find an excuse for our shortcomings. Often, we blame someone close to us because it is psychologically unpalatable to blame ourselves. A favorite whipping boy of investors is the broker or trading advisor. Every year there are hundreds if not thousands of frivolous lawsuits against brokers. I believe many of them are merely customers seeking revenge for their own bad investment decisions. This is not to say that all suits against brokers are without merit; however, I suspect that at least 75 percent of actions taken against brokers have no substance in fact.

This tendency works on a broader scale as well. When markets rally there is no shortage of individuals ready and willing to take credit for having called the move correctly. When markets top there are many who claim that they correctly foresaw the move. On the other hand, there are also those who are unable to admit they made a mistake. They conjure up any number of excuses, which can run the gamut from blaming the Federal Reserve, institutional traders, market specialists and pit brokers to writers of investment newsletters. There are literally hundreds of excuses. Each market has its favorite whipping boy.

Although the seeds of destruction for the greatest bull market in history are now being sown and are taking firm root, the odds are that when the financial bomb finally hits its mark, few will place the blame appropriately. Rather, they will look for the nearest, closest and most obvious cause. In this case, it will be the Y2K demon. I'll elaborate on this later, but now, I'd like to demonstrate that there are numerous factors, the most important of which relate to economic cycles and interest rates, that may ultimately result in a severe financial panic. While the panic may be precipitated by Y2K problems, *the true underlying reasons will have very little to do with Y2K.*

Significant Patterns

Consider the fact that since 1984 interest rates in the United States have declined persistently and steadily. As this book was being written (in late 1998), long-term interest rates reached their lowest level in many years. It is no surprise, therefore, that the stock market has reached its highest level in many years. As I pointed out earlier, while the relationship between stock price trends and interest rates is not always this predictable, it has been highly reliable historically.

Furthermore, short-term interest rates have also dropped substantially during this period. In the early 1990s short-term interest rates were at about the same level as they were in the early 1960s, well before the large upward move in interest rates that culminated in the early 1980s. As this example demonstrates, interest rate trends are a major force in the direction of economies and markets. What, how and when actions are taken to regulate interest rates can and do have a significant impact on markets both on a long-term and on a short-term basis.

While the direction and magnitude of interest rates are not the sole determinants of economic trends, they have played a major role in the past and probably will continue to be a major force. It behooves every serious investor to understand a few basic and important patterns. Knowing these patterns will not only help your long-term perspective on the markets and the economy, but the knowledge will also serve you well in making major investment decisions such as when to refinance a mortgage, when to buy or sell a home, or when to buy or sell gold, art, collectibles, and so on.

Summary

The role of interest rates both as indicator of economic strength and as a primary determinant of economic direction is undeniable. The role of government in controlling and regulating economies by controlling interest rates has grown substantially since the 1950s. As a consequence, most stock and commodity markets tend to move up and down with interest rates. If you are able to discern major moves in interest rates before they happen, then you possess a major key to successful trading and investing.

INTEREST RATE PATTERNS, CYCLES AND PRICES

Market analysis can be based on either an understanding of fundamental cause and effect or purely on observation without knowledge of underlying causes. The fundamental view of economies and markets seeks to find causes, using deductive reasoning to forecast and explain events.

> A year 2000 breakdown could do incalculable damage to investors' finances and could undermine their confidence in our entire financial structure.
> —Arthur Leavitt, Jr., Chairman, Securities and Exchange Commission

My approach focuses more on the relationship between events than on their underlying causes. If, for example, I can demonstrate that a given market relationship has occurred frequently over time, then future instances of these events should be fairly predictable. Many times the reasons for or causes of events are either unclear or unknown at the time the events occur. The relationships discussed in this chapter may not seem entirely logical when looked at simply from the standpoint of cause and effect. This does not, however, mean that they are not valid or that they are not effective tools for investing, analyzing markets or preparing one's financial future.

One of the more reliable relationships found in economic data is that between interest rates and various commodity prices. My research strongly suggests that we can develop reasonably accurate and effective forecasts by studying this relationship.

Take a few minutes to examine Figures 4.1 through 4.6. They show the relationship between long-term interest rates and various commodity prices. Although the relationship is not always exact, the overall trend of prices tends to be similar to that of interest rates. Yet, there are several notable exceptions to this general rule. We can learn a great deal about markets and economies by studying the exceptions:

Copper prices and long-term interest rates.   From 1864 through 1998, these have shown a close relationship. As you can see from Figure 4.1, the correlation is not 100 percent. The highs and lows do not line up exactly. At times copper prices peak and bottom before interest rates do and at times interest rates lead copper prices. But, looking at the big picture, the relationship holds, overall.

There are times, however, when copper prices and interest rates have gone their separate ways. A notable divergence occurred during the economic contraction (i.e., depression) of the 1930s. From 1948 to the late 1990s the patterns have generally trended in the same direction. In the late 1990s, copper prices as well as interest rates are relatively low. This situation is essentially similar to that of the mid-1960s. As a result, it would not be unrealistic to expect higher interest rates as well as higher copper prices in the near future. This suggests inflation. The low cost of money combined with low copper prices tends to fuel price rallies.

Petroleum prices and long-term interest rates.   Figure 4.2 shows the very clear and virtually one-to-one relationship between these two in the United States from 1939–1998. The peaks, troughs and trends are correlated very strongly. As you will note, both interest rates and petroleum prices are currently low. The situation is, in fact, even more significant than it was in the late 1970s when petroleum prices were low but interest rates were considerably higher than they are today. What does it mean? To me it suggests that both interest rates and petroleum prices are apt to rise strongly in the years ahead, which also suggests inflation. The low cost of money combined with a strong economy and the low cost of fuel will likely cause an increase in consumption. This will, in turn, deplete supplies and force prices higher.

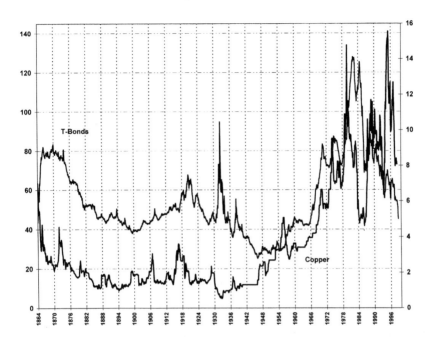

FIGURE 4.1   **Monthly Cash Average Copper vs. Monthly Average T-Bond Yields**
1864–1998

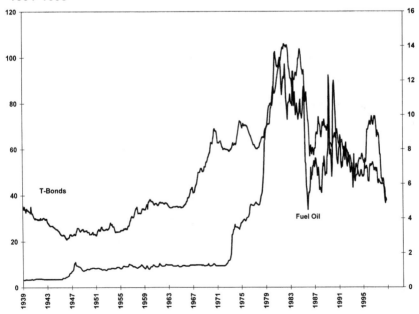

FIGURE 4.2   **Monthly Cash Average Fuel Oil vs. Monthly Average T-Bond Yields**
1939–1998

Long-term interest rates and soybean prices.   Figure 4.3 is another example of the relationship between commodity prices and interest rates. I cannot make a case for 100 percent correlation, since there are specific fundamental factors in soybean prices and in interest rates that are unique to each market. The general trends show striking similarities. In the late 1990s interest rates are at the same level they were when soybean prices were in the $3 range. From this we can conclude that the cost of money is cheap and that soybean prices are relatively cheap as well. Increased demand due to a growing economy will eventually absorb supply. The end result of this scenario may well be an explosive increase in soybean prices similar to what occurred in the 1970s. This, too, would be inflationary.

Coffee prices and interest rates.   Finally, consider Figure 4.4. While not so pronounced as the other examples, there is nevertheless a relationship. As you can see, today both coffee prices and interest rates are relatively low compared to their historical levels. The last time interest rates were this low, coffee prices were under 50 cents per pound. What, if anything, does this portend? To me it suggests the possibility of higher coffee prices, which would be an inflationary economic factor. Figures 4.5 and 4.6 show similar patterns in cash corn and beef steers versus bond yields.

We will return to these relationships in a later chapter, so please keep them in mind as you read on. There are other commodity markets that show similar correlations to interest rates. While I am not saying that interest rates are the determining factor, I am pointing out that there has long existed a close relationship between commodity prices, stock prices and interest rates. While this relationship is well known to professional traders, economists and market analysts, it is not one that most average investors recognize.

Nevertheless it is a highly important relationship that will be significant in the late 1990s and well beyond the Year 2000. It is interesting that the end of the millennium coincides with a low point in interest rates as well as in many commodity prices, and it is perhaps not coincidental that a low in interest rates, a record-high stock market (as of this writing) and the end of the millennium have all arrived at about the same time.

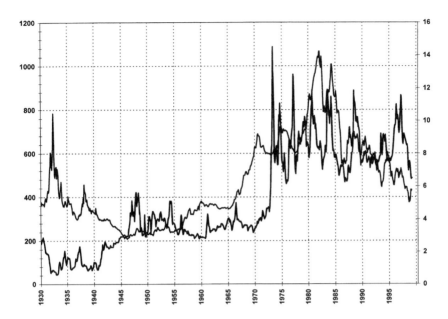

FIGURE 4.3   **Monthly Cash Average Soybeans vs. Monthly Average T-Bond Yields**
1930–1998

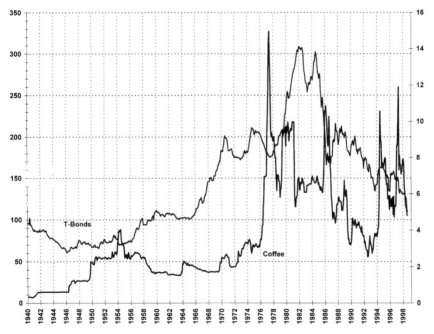

FIGURE 4.4   **Monthly Cash Average Coffee vs. Monthly Average T-Bond Yields**
1940–1998

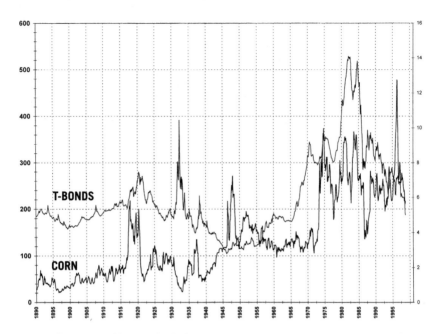

FIGURE 4.5   Monthly Cash Average Corn vs. Monthly Average T-Bond Yields
1890–1998

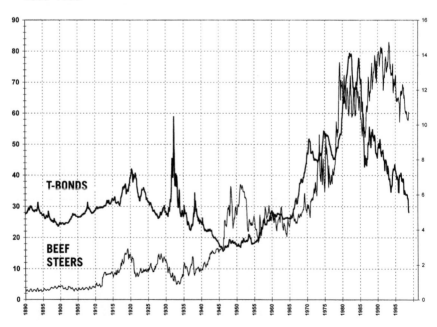

FIGURE 4.6   Monthly Cash Average Beef Steers vs. Monthly Average T-Bond
Yields 1890–1998

WAR AND ECONOMIC TURNS

There has been an uncanny (some say intentional) relationship between economic cycle lows in the United States and war. The so-called "bottom war" has always been a popular war in American history. Examples of bottom wars are the Spanish-American War, World War II and the Gulf War. The Spanish-American War ended the Depression of the late 1800s. Nearly 30 years later, World War II ushered in the end of the Great Depression and, in 1990, the Gulf War brought an end to the recession/depression of the 1980s. The bull market in stock prices that started in August 1991 correlated with the end of the Gulf War, and was not a random event. Looking back to the post World War II experience, we see essentially the same pattern.

I am not aware of any market forecaster who correctly predicted the length, strength or magnitude of the big stock market rally from the late 1980s through the end of the millennium. To do so would have required clairvoyance, a keen knowledge of economic history and the emotional fortitude necessary to withstand the almost certain storm of ridicule that would have followed such a forecast. To imply that the Dow Jones Industrial Average would attain the 10,000 level or higher by the end of the millennium would have been considered the height of sophistry, or at least an impossible outcome without hyperinflation.

Cyclical Price History

Although the vast majority of investors are ignorant of economic history, its lessons are painfully clear. American and European economies have experienced numerous periods of cyclical growth and contraction since the 1600s. Though not carbon copies of one another, each period of growth is characterized by essentially similar social, political, economic and religious themes. Each cycle or period followed a generally repetitive pattern of growth, crest, downturn and decay. Most of the "long-wave" economic cycles, as they have come to be called, measure approximately 50 to 60 years from start to finish. Although these economic cycles have been discussed in the writings of several economists, their theories are not generally accepted since they run contrary to more popular conceptions of economics.

The idea that economic history is relatively repetitive is unpalatable to those who feel that economic growth and contraction can be regulated and controlled to a certain extent. Indeed, the Great Depression posed a challenge to capitalist economic leaders. Specifically, the challenge was to forge an economy that discredited Marxist teachings while assuring once and for all that prosperity would be available to all citizens provided they were willing to work for it.

In spite of the seemingly obvious similarities shared by each cycle, the common threads could not be discerned in the heat of economic battle. An understanding of long-wave cycles can be acquired only by looking at the problem from a distance. Even the so-called "macro economists" were too entrenched in their theories to see the facts from afar. Except for a few brave souls whose work is still looked upon askance, the eyes of the world were too closely riveted on events to see trends. Each cyclical turn, particularly those that occurred in the 1970s and 1980s, took many of the "experts" by surprise.

VISUALIZING ECONOMIC TRENDS

Visualizing major economic trends is akin to viewing the works of great impressionist painters; they must first be studied from a distance. The blobs of color are interesting but seemingly random from close up. Yet from several yards away, they take on rich and flowing meaning. They transmit information to the senses and energy to the human brain. The parts become integrated in a greater whole. Once the total picture has been experienced, the viewer can step closer, closer and closer still without losing the meaning of the whole. The once seemingly random parts take on new life. What at first glance was meaningless acquires new and subtle definition upon each successive examination. The cyclical view of socioeconomic life is, in many respects, like the work of impressionist painters.

Although the lessons of economic history were clear, there were those who were either standing too close to see or too far away to see; those who were too biased to see; and those who were altogether blind. When the U.S. economy embarked on its long-term cyclical upswing in the 1950s, it was the general impression that new challenges were soon to be encountered. The impression was correct!

What many failed to realize was that the coming years would bring a replay of previous issues and trends. The story would be the same; only the names of the players would change. The lessons of economic history repeat. We need only learn from them if we are to enjoy success and prosperity.

Almost 58 years later came yet another "day of reckoning." On October 16, 1987, the Dow Jones stock average lost more than one hundred points. Following a weekend during which traders and investors had time to ponder the market's recent losses, Standard and Poor's futures opened sharply lower on Monday, October 19. The decline seemed, at first, to be a reasonable follow-through for a Monday after a weak Friday. However, within several hours after market openings, there were bargains galore. Adding to the panic was the eerie fact that the stock market crash of 1929 had also occurred in October. Investors, fearing a similar decline, sold stocks *en masse*. Panic selling followed.

A market maker at the Chicago Board Options Exchange told me "when the Dow was down 100 points we thought prices were cheap; we started buying. When the Dow was down 200 points we bought more. When it was down 300 we got worried. At 400 points lower we liquidated our positions and took the losses. We watched the last 100-plus point decline totally mesmerized, anesthetized by the avalanche of sellers, the lack of liquidity and the worst selling panic in stock market history."

Yes, in spite of the litany that "it can't happen again," it did. Ignoring the charts, the buyers, the speculators, the government and the bargain hunters, the beast of Wall Street unleashed a market purge that shook financial institutions worldwide to their very core. Those of us who had been preaching and warning about the coming decline were vindicated, but concerned about the future. Would this crash lead to a depression similar to the one that followed the Crash of 1929? Could the U.S. government control the market decline and the potential panic? Would a chain reaction of bankruptcies be the outcome of this new crash?

Based on the behavior of the U.S. economy and the stock market subsequent to the Crash of 1987, it is clear that underlying economic strength saved the market. Stocks went on to make major gains as the U.S. economy continued to be strong. Yet, in spite of all the strength in stocks from 1987 through 1999, a number of key factors and events are now all heading in the direction of a new and potentially frightening market decline. Among the factors are:

A change in the long-term cycle of interest rates.   Based on the 50- to 60-year cycle in U.S. long-term interest rates, the market is overdue for a major change in direction. My work suggests that interest rates are at a low point and that in the very near future they will begin to rise. The cycle suggests that interest rates could rise for a fairly long period of time. The increase in interest rates will make buying and holding stocks less attractive, thereby forcing stocks lower.

A change in the 4- and 8-year stock market cycles is now developing.   Ideally the market should peak by 2002; however, cyclical tops are less reliable and more difficult to forecast than are cyclical bottoms. The top could come as early as 2000 or as late as 2004. Regardless of when the market top actually occurs, we are now in a significant danger period during which the start of a major decline is possible.

Speculation in essentially worthless stocks continues to accelerate.   The Internet stock craze will eventually become a major "sucker play" in which millions of investors will lose record amounts of money.

Serious problems are anticipated due to Y2K computer failures.   These problems may be responsible for a top in the market and perhaps even in the U.S. economy, or the start of a severe decline. If the market has already peaked come Y2K and its attendant computer problems, then the market could drop further, based on Y2K panic selling.

A significant change in the overall trend of commodity prices is likely.   This change should begin before the Year 2000. This rise in commodity prices will likely be the first indication of a new inflationary trend. Such a trend will reduce profit margins, increase inflationary pressures and result in higher interest rates on an international basis.

These factors, coupled with intangible but potentially serious international political problems, could combine to exacerbate the situation.

Patterns and Cycles in Interest Rates

Capitalism is built on the concept of money making money. Hence, the availability of capital at low rates of interest tends to result in economic growth, whereas the burden of high interest rates tends to stifle economic growth. With high interest rates, and the concomitant disincentives to expansion, comes a decline in employment. The net result of lower employment is decreased earnings, greater government expense on social welfare programs and decreased national productivity. This highly oversimplified explanation will likely clot the blood of economists and rattle the bones of politicians. In reality, interest rates are sometimes a cause and at other times, an effect, having different impacts at different times in the cycle.

Although there are many explanations of how interest rates and money supply affect economies, my approach is a simple one: When the economy has been in a long-term decline, demand for goods and services has also been on the decline. During this period money is hard to come by. Concern on the part of consumers and businesses results in decreased levels of spending. Consumer goods that are not essential to survival are not purchased aggressively. Consumption, therefore, decreases markedly. There is usually a chain-reaction effect of decreased consumer activity; this results in lower employment because of the negative impact of decreased consumer activity on business and sales.

During declining economic trends, concern is reflected in high levels of saving and low levels of spending and consumption. This results in a relatively high level of cash and, therefore, lowers interest rates. A further downward stimulus on interest rates is the usual decrease in government borrowing. The end result is, therefore, a ready supply of money. Inasmuch as supply and demand are ingredients of price, the high relative supply of money and/or the low demand for money combine to force interest rates down.

All cycles eventually reach a point of equilibrium or, perhaps, a point at which prices are so low that demand is eventually stimulated. At economic lows, the cost of money becomes sufficiently low to foster an increase in demand that might not otherwise exist. This low cost of money becomes a cause. It has caused the consumer to act in response to a perceived opportunity. In other words, interest rates are so low that even the most skittish of investors or businesspersons are prompted to take action. In late 1998, interest rates were at or near such a low level. Even with the low profit margins and low consumer demand that accompany long-wave cyclic lows, demand will increase if the cost of doing business is low enough.

Concomitant with low interest rates, the low cost of raw materials and land are also stimuli for increased money demand. In other words, the equilibrium of price, cost of doing business and potential return has reached a level at which they stimulate increased business activity. This process often takes many years. All but the most astute investors stand aside during times of economic lows and deflation. Yet the best long-term business opportunities exist at the economic lows. When the overwhelming majority is unwilling to initiate or expand business, the shrewd investor is accumulating land, real estate, businesses and money at absurdly low prices. It's a buyer's market. You can almost name your price and get it. The current bottoming cycle of the late 1990s in U.S. interest rates could have a significant impact in association with Y2K problems.

LONG-TERM PATTERNS IN INTEREST RATES

Research by various economists and cyclical-market analysts has shown that long-term interest rates in the United States have fluctuated according to a number of repetitive patterns or cycles. Studying the cycles will not necessarily allow us to predict the level to which interest rates will go, but we can discern the following general information about interest rates:

- *Probable high or low time:* If we know when a cyclical pattern is due to peak or bottom, we can have a general idea of whether the interest rate market is close to a low or a high.
- *Probable direction:* If an interest rate cycle has peaked, then we can have a certain degree of confidence that the direction for a given period of time will be lower. If a cyclical low has been made, then we can forecast the approximate time length of the coming up-move.
- *Magnitude:* By knowing if a cycle is close to a peak or low, we also know if the price level is too high or too low. The ability to

evaluate magnitude or price level is the least reliable aspect of cyclical analysis.

The 54-year pattern.   There has been a pattern in long-term interest rates that has averaged approximately 54 years from one low point to the next. The last major low in interest rates was made in 1945, which means that 1999 should mark the approximate low of the current interest rate cycle if the pattern holds true. Figure 4.7 shows the last few repetitions of this pattern. As can be seen from the length across interest rate lows, the pattern is not perfect; however, it is sufficiently reliable to permit a forecast. Statisticians would argue (and correctly so) that the amount of historical data available for a valid long-term statistical analysis is limited and therefore that a statistically sound prediction about the 54-year interest rate cycle cannot be achieved due to this limitation. If, however, the cycle is now bottoming, then many capitalist economies throughout the world are likely to enter an extended period of inflation.

The approximate 9-to 11-year cycle in interest rates.   Figure 4.8 shows short-term U.S. interest rates, monthly average price, from 1893 through 1999. Short interest rates have shown a long-term cycle of approximately nine to eleven years, from low to low. The relative regularity of this cycle leads to the inevitable question: "Has Federal Reserve policy been an effective tool in controlling interest rates?" I'd say that if I knew nothing about the Federal Reserve and its actions, I certainly couldn't tell from the charts that any agency with significant power was attempting to control or regulate interest rates. Perhaps things might have been worse without the "Fed," yet the cycle lows and highs have most certainly not been significantly affected.

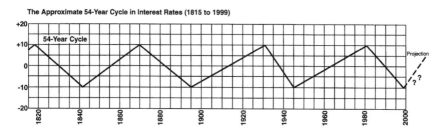

FIGURE 4.7   **Repetitions of the 54-Year Pattern in U.S. Interest Rates**

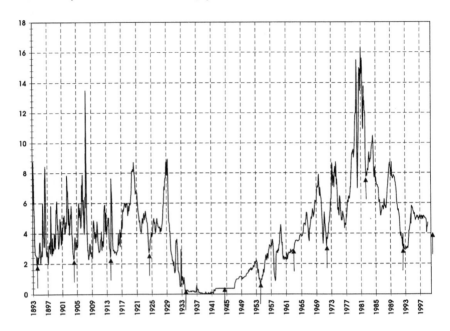

FIGURE 4.8 **Short-Term U.S. Monthly Average Interest Rate Yields from 1893 through 1999: 9- to 11-Year Cycle**

The 9- to 11-year cycle has been very reliable albeit not perfect. The last low occurred in the early 1990s with another low within the next few years. Note also that the 1992–1993 low was most likely a long-term (i.e., 54-year) low. The forecast is, therefore, for higher interest rates once the next low is in place.

The 9- to 11-year cycle in long-term U.S. interest rates. Long-term interest rate cycles have also shown a tendency for lows to occur about 9 to 11 years apart. Although this pattern has at times varied considerably from anticipated lows and highs, it is nonetheless a valid pattern. (See Figure 4.9.)

THE COMBINED CYCLE AND PATTERN INDICATIONS FOR LONG-TERM INTEREST RATES

Based on my studies, I would conclude:

1. Long-term interest rates have exhibited a long-wave cycle of from 50 to 60 years' duration, low to low. The next low point of

(x marks approximate lows)

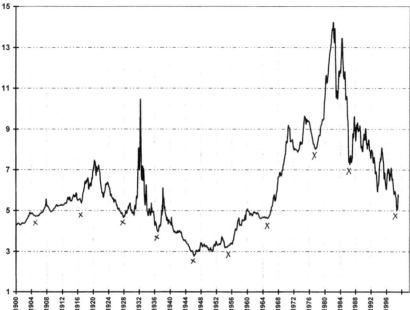

FIGURE 4.9   **Approximate Mid-Decade Lows in U.S. Interest Rates from 1906 through 1998**

this cycle was due in the late 1990s, and may already have been made. This suggests inflation.

2. Long-term interest rates since 1916 have exhibited a mid-to-late decade low tendency; therefore, it is likely that lows are already in place.

3. Each approximate 54-year cycle in long-term interest rates consists of approximately five 9- to 11-year cycles. We are now in the upward phase of these cycles.

4. Long-term interest rates made lows in 1843, 1899 and 1945. In each case the lows were made at or close to the time frame of long-wave (approximately 54 years) economic cycle lows. It is likely, therefore, that an inflationary cycle is now beginning.

5. Long-term interest rates made highs in approximately 1815, 1857, 1919, 1931 and 1981. Each top was in the same time frame as the long-wave economic peak or while the decline was in process. It is reasonable to assume that 1981 marked the last inflationary peak and that 1999 is the time frame during which a period of inflationary movement should begin.

6. Long-term interest rates since 1906 have shown a tendency to bottom toward the mid-portion of each decade and to peak late in the decade or early in the next decade. We are at or near that point.

7. Long-term interest rates since the early 1800s have shown a highly predictable and fairly symmetrical cycle of approximately 9 to 11 years from one low point to the next, with the shortest cycle being approximately 8 years and the longest being approximately 12 years. On average, the approximate 9-1/2-year time span has been fairly reliable and dependable. This suggests that interest rates in the late 1990s are at a relative low point and likely to move higher.

The 6-year pattern in interest rates.   There has also been an approximate 6-year pattern in interest rates as measured from one low point to the next. The best way to observe this pattern is by examining Figure 4.10. Note that the cycle has not been perfectly symmetrical. I have marked the last four tips with a heavy vertical line. The ideal cycle is shown at the bottom of the chart. Also notice a projected low in 2001. Since the futures market works opposite from cash yields, the projected low in futures is a projected high in the actual interest rate yield.

What the Cycles Suggest

My evaluation of the various interest rate cycles strongly suggests that the era of "cheap money" is at an end. It is very likely that we are about to embark on a lengthy period of higher interest rates. The stimuli for higher rates could be a combination of the following fundamental causes:

1. The U.S. Federal Reserve moves to raise interest rates in an effort to curb rampant day trading and highly speculative trading in essentially worthless stocks. Such actions would be reminiscent of government attempts to control speculative stock activity prior to and during the Stock Market Crash of 1929.

2. Low interest rates and strong economic growth combine to create strong demand for loans, thereby forcing rates higher.

3. A new cycle uptrend in commodity prices forces increased borrowing and thereby stimulates higher interest rates.

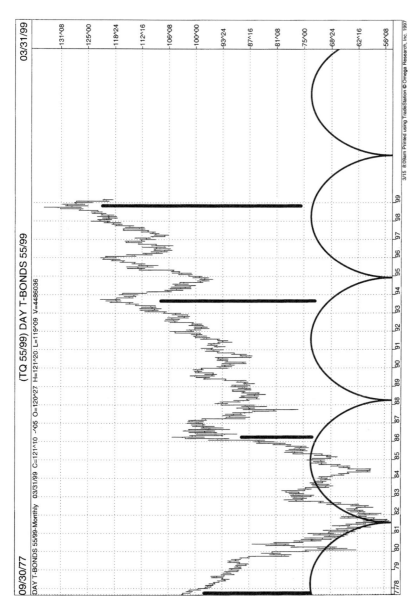

FIGURE 4.10 The Approximate 6-Year Cycle in T-Bond Futures (Chart created with TradeStation® 2000i by Omega Research, Inc.) ©1997 Omega Research, Inc.

65

4. A sharp increase in demand for cash due to Y2K-inspired hoarding forces higher interest rates.

In the event that any or all of the above (along with other factors)
prompt a new upmove in interest rates, it is very likely that inflation-
sensitive investments could serve as a good hedge against declining
stock markets.

The Long Wave

The remote Siberian tundra is home to the remains of Nikolai D.
Kondratieff, the Russian renegrade economist of the 1920s.
Kondratieff, who in 1926 wrote *Die Langen Wellen der Konjunktur**
(Long Waves in Economic Life), would have regarded the developing
low in interest rates as compelling evidence that his theory was correct. But before his work had progressed to its final proof, Kondratieff
was exiled to Siberia because his theories contradicted Marxist ideology. Without solid statistical validation, Kondratieff's long-wave economic theories were criticized, ridiculed and rejected, not only by his
Soviet leaders but also by economists the world over. With the exception of a few contemporary market analysts and/or economists, the
long-wave theories of Kondratieff have received limited attention or
constructive contemporary research.

Those of us who have studied cycles in prices, economics, history
and political and social science have little doubt that long-wave economic cycles are real, reliable and predictable. There is ample statistical evidence that most stock and commodity markets move in predictable and demonstrable cycles and patterns. Although this premise
is still not widely accepted by economists, politicians or the investing
public, the fact that economic history has repeated itself—not once or
twice, but many times—is difficult to dismiss. Those who know the
cycles and, moreover, their ramifications, are not surprised by even the
most extreme of economic events. Rather, they are prepared well in
advance to survive and, perhaps, even profit during times of economic chaos and disruption.

---

* Kondratieff, N. D., "Die Langen Wellen der Konjunktur," *Archiv fur Sozialwissenschaft und
Sozialpolitik,* Vol. 56, 1926, pp. 573–609.

The works of Kondratieff and other cyclical economists such as Schumpeter, Kitchin and Juglar lead me to the following conclusions, all of which are based on the fact that history in economies and markets repeats. While the history may not be exactly the same, there are common threads underlying repetition.

I believe that the following facts and conclusions are warranted:

- The history of prices and price trends in many markets is repetitive and, within limits, predictable;

- Major trends are more readily predictable than specific prices;

- The ability to forecast the approximate timing of a given event or events is considerably more important than the ability to predict or forecast the exact price of a top or bottom in any given market or economy;

- Economic fluctuations are influenced by cyclical price fluctuations, mass psychology and social, political and religious phenomena;

- Capitalist economies fluctuate in cyclical movements, the most important of which are the "long waves";

- Long-wave economic cycles, like all cycles, consist of several specific stages or phases;

- There are numerous social, political and religious correlatives to each economic phase or stage; and

- There are various strategies, investment alternatives and preparatory actions that investors and businesspeople can take in anticipation of and in preparation for the various long-wave cycle stages.

The Interest Rate Top of the Early 1980s

The interest rate peak of the early 1980s is an excellent example of how interest rate cycles can and do exert a major influence on stock and commodity prices. From 1970 to 1982 the U.S. economy experienced a period of strong growth and inflationary pressures. Commodity prices rose across a broad front. (Figures 4.11, 4.12 and 4.13 show how corn and cattle prices rose substantially during this period of time.) In order to put the brakes on what was considered excessive growth and inflationary pressures, the U.S. Federal Reserve

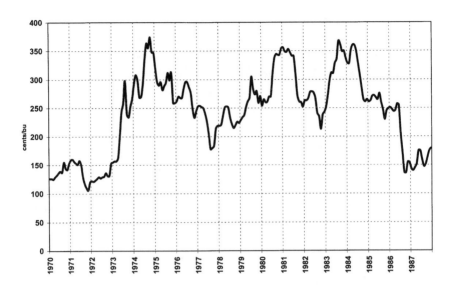

FIGURE 4.11   **The Rise in Corn Prices from 1970 through 1984**

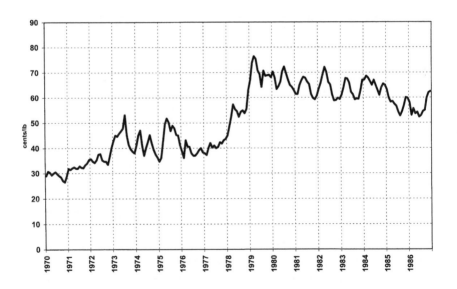

FIGURE 4.12   **The Rise in Cattle Prices from 1970 through 1979**

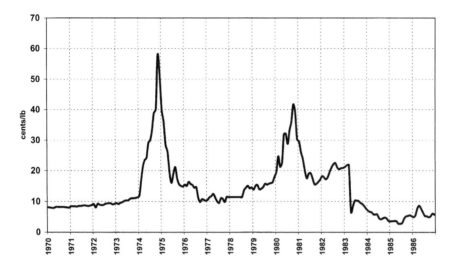

FIGURE 4.13   The Rise in Sugar Prices from 1970 through 1974 and from 1977 through 1980

raised interest rates steadily and concertedly until they reached a point where excessive borrowing was thwarted and many commodity prices began to decline. Before long, real estate prices fell sharply, commodity prices dropped and banks began to fail in a chain reaction of poor liquidity resulting from defaults on loans. Personal and corporate bankruptcies rose sharply as the U.S. economy contracted.

THE SILVER LINING

As interest rates continued to decline, investors and money managers realized that there was only one logical and reasonably "safe" place for their money. Yields on common stocks outstripped what could be had in savings accounts, Treasury bills and Treasury bonds. Slowly at first, money that might have been placed in bonds, T-bills and commercial paper found its way into the stock market. Increased demand for stocks drove prices higher.

At the same time, interest rates continued their decline. The cost of borrowing money to finance business expansion declined, creating a favorable business climate. Consumers watched their cost of borrowing decline steadily. Attracted by the low cost of money, consumers began to spend and to accumulate credit card debt. The ability to finance plastic debt with low interest rates was a further motivator. Demand for goods and services increased, stimulating corporate profits which, in turn, sent stocks higher. Encouraged by higher stocks and a favorable business climate, investors bought more stocks.

The Federal Reserve, still unconcerned about any excesses in economic growth, continued with their policy of stable and declining interest rates. From 1981 to 1993 Treasury bill yields declined steadily to levels that had not been seen since the early 1960s. The cycle continued as lower interest rates and a positive attitude by the Federal Reserve boosted consumer confidence. The game continued. The declining trend in interest rates from 1982 through 1999 correlated almost exactly with the rising trend in stock prices during the same period of time. Figure 4.14 shows this strong correlation.

FIGURE 4.14   The Correlation of Short-Term Interest Rates and Stock Prices 1976 through 1999

Summary

The direction of stock prices in the United States is inextricably related to the direction of interest rates. This is a result of Federal Reserve policies directed at controlling markets, prices and economic trends. When interest rates are declining, stocks are usually rallying. When interest rates become excessively high and investors can lock in a virtually guaranteed return by investing in Treasury bonds, stocks are unattractive. However, when interest rates are low, investors and money managers are attracted to stocks, provided that yields (that is, dividends) are higher than what may be achieved in interest-bearing vehicles. This relationship has been a primary driving force behind stock prices since 1982 as it was during many previous stock market rallies and declines.

The major trend in the U.S. stock market has been up since the long-term interest rate peak in 1982. Therefore, an upturn in U.S. interest rates could very well correlate with a stock market decline. Based on the high probability that U.S. interest rates are likely to turn higher for an extended period of time, the odds favor a stock market decline. Given the far-reaching and significant implications of a major change in the direction of interest rates, I have concluded that:

- Although long-term interest rates between 1995 and 1999 have been in an area of major lows, a number of cycles are now coming into play that will likely result in short-term as well as long-term increases in interest rates. Based on the shorter-term cycles, the trend of interest rates is likely to be higher for several years and, based on the longer-term cycles and patterns in interest rates, the rise is likely to continue for as long as 15 years. The anticipated rise in interest rates will likely have a negative effect on stock prices and could very well put pressure on stock prices for a number of years, particularly once the rise in interest rates begins in earnest. The correlation of a rise in interest rates, a possible top in stocks and the Year 2000 is most likely coincidence but nonetheless significant.

- At first the expected increase in interest rates may be relatively slow inasmuch as the Federal Reserve will want to avoid creating a panic. However, if inflationary pressures become too severe or intense, then large rate increases can be expected.

- The increase in interest rates will not affect stock prices if stocks continue to maintain yields that are high relative to interest rates.

However, should interest rates rise sharply, stocks could decline sharply as investors and money managers seek a higher return and safe haven for their money. Yields could be significantly affected by a rise on raw commodity prices that will reduce corporate profit margins.

■ Should interest rates remain relatively stable, rising only slowly, then the U.S. stock market can continue its rise.

■ In order to maintain high price levels, corporate profits and dividends will need to grow steadily. Unless such growth can be sustained, stocks will decline, possibly with considerable force and magnitude. Consider the possibility that large expenditures on Y2K readiness could cut deeply into corporate profits of major firms. In recent months it has become clear that the cost of Y2K preparation is much larger than originally anticipated. Consider also the impact of potential business losses to firms that are not Y2K ready.

■ The longer U.S. interest rates remain low, the more likely an increase in the rate of inflation. Once there are signs of inflation, the U.S. Federal Reserve will raise interest rates. Depending upon the manner and extent of the interest rate rise, the U.S. as well as world stock markets will be affected either minimally or substantially.

■ Investors are urged to become interest rate watchers. Look for signs and symptoms that the interest rate trend is about to reverse itself. This will be abundantly clear from changes in Federal Reserve policy. It will also be clear from an assessment of the interest rate futures markets, which are sensitive to developing changes in the direction of interest rates.

■ The history of interest rates in the United States is very clear and highly repetitive. There is no reason to believe that the patterns in interest rates have changed or that the market has ceased to be cyclical. They are one of the key driving forces in the boom-and-bust economic trends and they are the key driving force in the rise and fall of stock prices.

■ Increased demand for cash and credit as a result of Y2K concerns and/or panic hoarding of cash due to Y2K hysteria could easily drive interest rates higher due to increased demand and government action to curb unnecessary borrowing.

■ Commodity prices for fuel, grains and other foods could also rise due to consumer hoarding. Such a rise in prices could easily result in a chain reaction of price increases.

ECONOMIC CYCLES: NINE STAGES FROM GROWTH TO PEAK TO REBIRTH

In order to understand why the Year 2000 crisis could result in a severe economic collapse (even if it is a brief one), we must first understand the nature of economic stages. All markets and economies pass through approximately nine stages during their "life." Each stage

Many persons think that by hoarding money they are only gaining safety for themselves. If money is your only hope for independence, you will never have it. The only real security that a man can have in this world is a reserve of knowledge, experiences and ability. Without these qualities, money is practically useless. The security even of money depends on knowledge, experience and ability. If productive ideas are displaced by destructive ideas, economic life suffers.

—Henry Ford

has its unique characteristics. Here is a summary of these stages. (Please refer to Figure 5.1 for an illustration of the ideal stages, and to Figure 5.2 for a look at the gold market in terms of these stages.) Note that these stages can be applied to an economy or to a given market.

Remember, the various scenarios presented here are strictly ideals. No single long-wave economic cycle will conform to the ideal stages 100 percent of the time. In the most recent cycle, for example, there were some fairly long periods of time that did not conform precisely to expectations of the ideal model. In 1958, a year during which Stage 2 growth was supposed to be occurring, the economy was weak. The

STAGE 1   The Initial Growth Stage
      2   The Secondary Growth Stage
      3   The Rapid Acceleration and Inflationary Increase Stage
      4   The "Blowoff" Peak Stage
      5   The Initial Decline
      6   The Recovery Period
      7   Gradual Decline and the Start of Secondary Depression
      8   Extended Decline
      9   Base Building

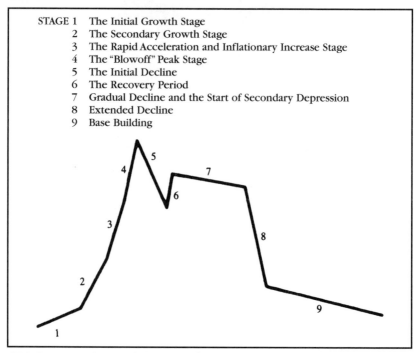

FIGURE 5.1   Stages of the Economic Cycle

purpose of this analysis is to provide a structure that will help you recognize long-wave economic cycle phases.

If you understand the ideal structure and aspects of each cyclic phase, you will be able to evaluate each situation individually, to distinguish what is merely a temporary deviation from a more serious or lasting divergence from the long-term trend. To an analyst familiar with these stages, the weak economy of the late 1950s and early 1960s would have been seen as a temporary phase, one likely to reverse itself within several years as prices returned to their upward trend in line with the long-wave cycle.

Stage 1: Initial Growth

During this stage of the economic cycle, growth is rather slow. There is a tendency for prices to be low as a carryover from the previous cycle bottom. In the case of a given stock or market, price is relatively low compared with where it had been in recent years. If the cycle

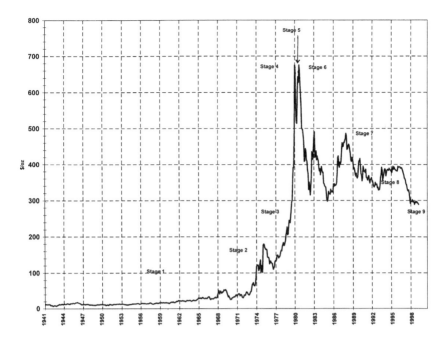

FIGURE 5.2   **Monthly Gold Index and Cash Gold: Nine Stages of the Long-Term Cycle**

being analyzed is an economic wave, then there are a number of specific correlates: social, political and economic. On the economic level, interest rates tend to be low, and commodity and stock prices are frequently low (*low* will be more specifically defined later). My economic comments in the analyses refer primarily to long-wave economic cycles of approximately 50 to 60 years, low to low.

Real estate and land prices tend to be down as well. Economic indicators such as the Gross National Product (GNP), Producer Price Index (PPI) and Wholesale Price Index (WPI) also tend to be lower than they had been in previous stages. Unemployment may still be relatively high as a carryover from the economic low period that immediately precedes this phase. Value of the dollar (or currency) is still high in comparison with foreign currencies and as a carryover of the economic low period that typically precedes Stage 1.

Government is usually emerging from a conservative period and entering a more liberal phase. The succession of presidents and congressional composition from economic low periods to the initial growth stage is usually one of conservatism to liberalism. During the previous economic low period, government has usually been forced to become more pro-business and liberal simply to improve business incentives; this, in turn, stimulates employment and, therefore, the economy in general. Business incentives increase, tax liability decreases, regulations are relaxed and controls are reduced across a broad front.

Social attitudes are slow to become more liberal. In the current period, such things as negative attitudes toward birth control, strict abortion laws and racial discrimination, tend to continue as they did during the previous economic decline. Very gradually there is a move toward relaxation of conservative attitudes and opinions. In addition, a gradual decline in religious practice begins to develop.

The direction set into motion during the last stage of the previous cycle and Stage 1 of the current cycle tends to continue. To a certain extent, it would be possible to determine the current stage of a long-term cycle merely by examining the major social, political and economic issues at any given point in time. (This will become more evident as you read further.)

Stage 2: Expansion and Secondary Growth

In the case of a specific stock or other type of market, the secondary growth or expansion phase is marked by an expansion of price range. In other words, prices begin to fluctuate more widely. Stock and futures price movements are generally larger from one time period to the next (day to day or week to week), and the amount of participation, or trading volume, increases as more investors are drawn to the market. This shows an increase in demand, which is usually followed by an increase in price, assuming that supply lags behind increasing demand.

Expansion and broader participation in the business and public sectors also characterize this stage of the long-wave economic cycle.

The public is not generally concerned with inflation, as growth is slow and steady. Unemployment has usually started to decrease, and interest rates are slowly beginning to inch higher along with GNP (Gross National Product), PPI (Producer Price Index) and CPI (Consumer Price Index). Capital available for borrowing at reasonably low rates is plentiful. Expansion in virtually any industry is possible at a reasonable cost. Social attitudes begin to liberalize gradually.

Government is still responsive and friendly to business; however, the initial seeds of labor discontent are now being sown. Yet Stage 2 does not assure economic growth. There have been periods of economic contraction during Stage 2. This stage can be, and has been, somewhat unpredictable. Considerable economic "push–pull" is typical in Stage 2, and recessions are not uncommon.

During this stage, and during the latter portion of Stage 1, the role of scientific innovation becomes particularly important. In the 1950s, for example, atomic power and a variety of chemical processes that were developed in the latter part of the 1930s' Depression era became important in industrial development. Rocket technology, developed during World War II, became the core of the American and Soviet space programs. Some theorists have suggested that scientific innovations are the stimulus for new economic growth.

In general, this stage offers long-term investors the most promising opportunities. This is when real estate, stock, land and most businesses offer "ground floor" opportunities. The potential for profit is greater than it was in Stage 1. The cost of doing business is still sufficiently low to permit a variety of opportunities. Yet, in spite of what seems to be reasonably obvious, all but the most visionary individuals are unwilling to take risks. They would rather wait until "things are clearly better" to take a chance. By the time success appears more certain, however, there is more risk and the economic peak is closer. Most individuals are still recovering from recent losses and extended economic contraction. They are unwilling to take risk without clear and virtually guaranteed success.

It is also during this stage that social mores, attitudes and opinions begin to move in a more liberal direction. The seeds of liberal social movements are often sown. (In the last Stage 2, sexual revolution, equal rights, self-awareness, alternate religious practice and truly free speech prevail.)

Stage 3: Rapid Acceleration and Inflationary Increase

Inflation becomes a more serious issue in Stage 3 as virtually all prices begin to increase. Labor gains a significant amount of power, while business continues to expand. Labor begins to have less buying power despite higher wages due to inflation; and there is more labor discontent as well as an increase in union membership. Unions begin to wield more power. Business makes concessions to labor, since profits are expanding, and it needs workers to meet demand for its products. Every day lost from the job is a day of lost profits. Therefore, negotiations are quick, and labor gets most of what it wants. Everybody seems to get what he or she wants at the expense of the consumer. Issues begin to heat up. Labor continually wants more, while industry begins to feel that too much is being taken by greedy workers.

As commodity prices continue to rise during this stage, profit margins decrease. Business leaders soon realize that they have painted themselves into a corner. They cannot cut costs by paying less for their raw products. They must pay whatever the market demands. Even if they have done an excellent job of purchasing their goods in advance at lower prices, they will eventually need to come into the open market to buy more goods. Wholesale prices remain high. Wages cannot be significantly reduced, or unions will call for a strike. Employees cannot be laid off or fired; the unions have become too strong. Industry has no choice but to once again pass increased costs along to the consumer. Consumers begin to feel the pinch. They demand higher wages, and again business is squeezed for more money. The vicious cycle continues.

On a social level, however, discontent continues to grow. Liberal movements tend to adopt anti-establishment attitudes. The split between social classes becomes more severe. Ethnic groups are more willing to express their discontent. Factions of all sorts begin to demonstrate in favor of their individual causes.

Political developments are also significant. Government has become ultra-liberal, taking on massive debt through social welfare programs, national improvement programs, and increased military spending. Government goes into debt by printing more money, but this is not necessarily the evil that will ultimately cause serious economic woes. Rather, a combination of factors and events will take their toll.

If past is prologue, the seeds of war are being sown. Slowly but surely, nations are beginning to prepare for war as international conflict and tensions mount. Each long-wave cycle in the U.S. economy has been marked by a so-called "top war." Top wars since the 1790s have been the War of 1812, the Civil War, World War I, and the Vietnam War. As you can see, not all of the top wars have been international in scope. Yet they have all had one element in common in addition to conflict, killing and destruction: They have all been unpopular wars—

wars that were not generally supported by the public. The timing of top wars is not precise, but they tend to come close to the top of the economic cycle.

The behavior of stocks or other markets (as opposed to an economy) is less complex during Stage 3. During this stage in the cycle, prices begin to accelerate rapidly. The momentum of a given stock, commodity or market increases rapidly. Typically, public opinion is exceptionally positive or bullish regarding the future. Upon close examination of price, however, the analyst will clearly see that inflation has taken hold, that price and underlying value are clearly out of adjustment, that value is much lower than price. Still, there is sufficient momentum to force prices higher. Reason, good sense, rational economics and conservative investment planning take a back seat to mob psychology, greed and the fear of being left out of a major upmove in prices.

Stage 4: The "Blowoff"

The key features of this stage are panic buying, very rapid price increases and peaks in many segments of the economy. This is the most dramatic of times in many years. Events worldwide and domestically are moving at a rapid pace. It seems as if everything affects the economy. In fact, a crisis is developing. On a political level, governments, which typically are liberal at or during the blowoff top, are followed by a more conservative government after the top.

During Stage 4, society is also in a state of considerable agitation. There is often marked polarization of attitudes and opinions. In the early 1970s, for example, just prior to the blowoff peak in commodity prices, there were "hard-hat riots" on Wall Street. American workers attacked students whom they viewed as liberals or radicals who favored changes. The workers perceived the changes as a threat to their recently found prosperity. Affluence, and the threat or fear of its withdrawal, brings about tensions. As it becomes clear that prosperity may end—because of reckless government policies, high interest rates or high retail prices—public protests increase, and with them social unrest.

It does not necessarily follow, however, that stock market prices are at their peak in Stage 4. In fact, it has been fairly common for stocks to peak a number of years after peaks in commodity prices and the economy. A 1919–1921 peak in commodity prices preceded the 1929 peak in stock prices. A 1974 peak in commodity prices preceded the 1987 peak in stock prices.

The relationship among economic stages, the current stock market and the coming Y2K crisis, may not precisely match the ideal stages I've described. For a variety of reasons, world stock markets must be evaluated as entities somewhat separate from the underlying economic trend. There was a time when the stock market trend and the economic trend were closely related to one another without much lead or lag time. This seems to have changed dramatically during the current cycle. While the general relationships are still similar, the lead and lag time have likely changed substantially.

Stage 4 is the most dramatic and violent period in the long-wave cycle. Though there are many problems, concerns, fears and panics to follow, Stage 4, the blowoff, is the most volatile. A sense of the extreme price volatility associated with this stage can be seen in Figures 5.3 and 5.4, where the price volatility overshadows virtually everything seen for many years previous.

In terms of time, Stage 4, the "blowoff" top, tends to be rather short-lived. By virtue of the extreme emotionalism and speculation that accompany this stage, it is more violent than it is long lasting. During this stage, the investment world is in a state of great turmoil, turmoil that sets the trend for a number of years to come. Quick-fix solutions are sought and the economy is patched up and painted to look healthy. This is not because there are no solutions. Rather, it is because the solutions are not easily implemented and are often unpopular with the public.

Good health is not recaptured without pain. Physical aging in adults can frequently be retarded by the application of simple, well-known and sensible techniques. Diet, exercise, rest, a slower pace of living, vitamins, reduction of stress and so forth are obvious solutions, but their benefits are not realized without effort, time and a gradual but total change in lifestyle.

Economies age as well. Stage 4 marks the top of the growth phase and the beginning of the decline phase. The diets of the growth phase, its pace of life and its excesses have all come home to roost. The problems can be solved, but it takes austerity, rational economic policies, a slow but steady return to budget balance, slow but relentless eco-

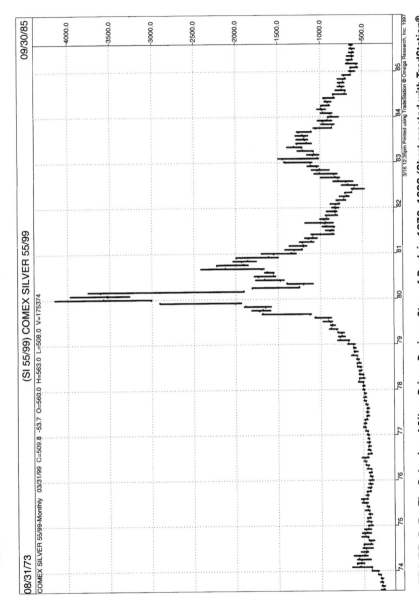

FIGURE 5.3 The Behavior of Silver Prices During a Stage 4 Peak in 1979–1980 (Chart created with TradStation® 2000; by Omega Research, Inc.) ©1997 Omega Research, Inc.

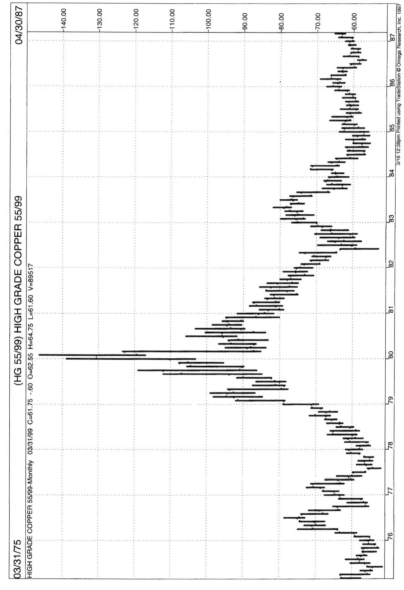

FIGURE 5.4   The Behavior of Copper Prices During a Stage 4 Peak in 1979–1980 (Chart created with TradStation® 2000; by Omega Research, Inc.) ©1997 Omega Research, Inc.

nomic contraction, a reasonable tax structure and sufficient incentives for business. A sound monetary policy is also of primary importance.

The cosmetic touch-ups initially applied will only work for so long. Eventually, the dike will collapse under the force of discontented waves and a tidal wave of illness. The structure will be demolished. At first, only bits and pieces will collapse. Water will rush in, destroying large segments of the structure. Investors and businesses caught in the deluge will either be destroyed or, if they are fast enough, will move out of the way. The chain reaction will eventually take its toll as wave after wave of seething waters rush in to threaten the stability of an already unsound structure.

With each wave, more and more businesses will fail. All social classes will suffer. Unemployment will increase and, eventually, what started as a trickle will end as a flood. The old will be buried, save for a few pillars of the past that will remain sufficiently stable to support a new foundation for a new structure. Stage 4 marks the start of deterioration. It is during this stage that investors, businesspeople and governments can take definitive actions that will save them. Unfortunately, they rarely do.

PROSPERITY DURING STAGE 4: RECOGNIZE THE SIGNALS

Figure 5.5 lists some symptoms and events that historical precedent suggests tend to characterize Stage 4.

Signal 1. Interest rates have reached record or near-record levels. This has been a result of record demand for money by government, business and the public. Take advantage of this opportunity to lock in a high rate of return on funds. The purchase of government bonds or other relatively "safe" vehicles is recommended. Note: There is also bound to be some question about the safety of banks during this crisis period. Therefore, it would be advisable to review the financial stability of any banking institution in which you have placed funds.

Signal 2. The various measures of inflation are all at or near record levels. This is a key indication that all is not well, that there are serious problems and that the time has come for many inflation-related investments (such things as precious metals, rare coins, objects

1. Interest rates tend to reach record levels with violent swings and immense volatility.
2. The rate of inflation, the Wholesale Price Index and the Consumer Price Index all tend to reach record high levels.
3. Most commodity markets peak in a dramatic fashion.
4. Demand for loans is at record levels.
5. There is growing concern for the stability and safety of banks.
6. Credit is hard to come by and businesses begin to fail.
7. There is consumer resistance to excessively high prices.
8. There is rampant speculation in virtually all markets and investments.
9. Domestic productivity is low while wages are high.
10. There are numerous stock and bond offerings.
11. Government begins to recognize that there may be a problem and begins to tighten spending.
12. Tighter government controls put further strain on an already taxed business sector.
13. To meet its own debt obligations, government seeks to raise taxes.
14. Economic slowdown begins to take hold toward the end of Stage 4.
15. The top war ends.
16. An initial disinflationary or recessionary decline develops.

FIGURE 5.5 **Characteristics of Stage 4**

d'art, most real estate and the like) to be liquidated. At this point in the long-wave cycle, a transition from intangible assets to tangible assets should take place, and your primary tangible asset should be cash.

Signal 3. A dramatic peak in commodity markets. The history of commodity price peaks is shown in Figure 5.6, which depicts the Commodity Research Bureau Futures Price Index before, during and after the current long-wave cyclic peak. Although some markets will make another peak over a period of several years following the Stage 4 top, most markets will decline precipitously.

This does not necessarily include the stock market. Stock prices tend to peak well after commodity prices. Regardless of which mar-

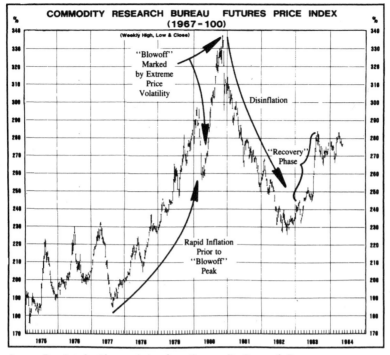

Source: Reprinted with permission from Commodity Research Bureau

FIGURE 5·6   Futures Price Index 1970–1990

kets peak first, the fact remains that this time frame is one during which tops are made in a great majority of the markets. It is vital that you be aware of the trend change and, above all, that you take action promptly and assertively.

Signal 4. Demand for money and loans is usually at record levels. This is also a very clear sign that the long-wave peak has arrived. Not only does government demand for money add to the problem, but the government makes it harder to get money by keeping interest rates high. The very high level of loan demand clearly indicates that all is not well. It suggests that business is suffering and that a credit crisis is in the making. Few signals or indicators of an economic peak are as reliable or telltale as this one. Do not ignore it!

Signal 5. Growing concern for the stability of banks. Typically, banks are loaned to their maximum, and there is concern about the ability of many lenders to repay loans. During the current long-wave cycle, foreign governments have been the largest borrowers unable to repay loans. In addition, farm loan payments have been in jeopardy, thereby placing considerable strain on the stability of rural banks. The credit situation tends to deteriorate even more after Stage 4 is over. Bank failures increase. The 1983–1987 time period witnessed a record number of bank failures.

Signal 6. Credit is difficult to obtain.   Banks tighten their requirements and reach their lending limits. The demand for credit is so high that banks are loath to take additional credit risks. Their requirements are more stringent, and their willingness to take on unnecessary risk is diminished because of concern about the ability of many borrowers to repay loans. There are clear indications that a banking crisis is developing. You should be aware of the developing crisis and act accordingly.

Signal 7. Consumer resistance to excessively high prices.   This resistance eventually stimulates the decline and causes the initial wave of selling.

Signal 8. Rampant speculation in virtually all markets and investments.   The most recent economic peak (prior to the 1987 crash) was marked by wild speculation in futures, land, precious metals, strategic metals and stocks. (In fact, the stock market peak of 1987 was preceded by a peak of commodity prices a number of years earlier, repeating the scenario of the previous—1920s—economic peak.)

Signal 9. Domestic productivity is low; wages are high.   This situation continues to plague businesses in the United States even in 1999, while foreign productivity remains high with wages relatively low.

Signal 10. Stock and bond offerings are plentiful.   This was true prior to the 1987 Stock Market Crash, and this scenario mimics similar situations during previous long-wave peaks.

Signal 11. Government begins to tighten spending.   Although deficit spending is clearly recognized as a problem, the alternative, which is a balanced budget, is unpalatable but necessary.

Signal 12. Tighter government controls are enacted.   This puts further strain on an already overburdened business sector. Bureaucracy continues to plague business, further increasing its inefficiency. The net result is a further strain on the productivity and profitability of U.S. businesses.

Signal 13. Government seeks to raise taxes.   This, of course, comes as no surprise to any student of economic history. It is not until the destructive effect of excessively high taxes is recognized that changes are made.

Signal 14. Economic slowdown begins to take hold.   This occurs toward the end of Stage 4. Figure 5.6 best illustrates what happens.

Signal 15. The top war comes to an end.   This initially brings optimism, but it signals the start of an important disinflationary trend.

Signal 16. A disinflationary or recessionary decline develops.

Stage 5: The Initial Decline

Following Stage 4, a period of initial decline tends to occur. The decline, like the one after the 1980 peak, can be quite severe; however, it is usually seen as a welcome relief to inflation. Stage 5 should be seen as a warning sign that all is not well and that the long-wave decline probably has started. At this point, debt reduction is perhaps the single most important thing that the average individual can do.

The initial decline comes in response to the top war. (Stage 5 recessions have occurred in the U.S. economy after the Seven Years War [approximately 1766], The War of 1812, the Civil War, World War I and the Vietnam War.) However, Stage 5, the initial decline, is more than a mere reaction to the excesses of the top war and the period of inflation that usually precedes it. It has almost always been a harbinger of deflation, a warning that the economic top has been seen, an advance indication that investors should prepare for bad times ahead—times that will ultimately end in the "bottom war." But well before the bottom war, a period of panic, disinflation and/or depression is likely to occur.

Stage 6: Recovery Period/Top Test

In the U.S. economy, it has been typical for a period of recovery to follow the initial decline of Stage 5. A recession followed the Seven Years
War, after which a period of recovery preceded the American
Revolution. A Stage 6 recovery was also seen after the War of 1812. The
Era of Good Feelings was a Stage 6 recovery, as was the Reconstruction
period following the Civil War. The "Roaring '20s" recovery followed
the 1920 economic peak and the greatest bull market in American history followed the economic peak of approximately 1974.

During the period of recovery, or top test, government becomes
acutely aware of the existing economic crisis. At this point, the economic malaise has usually become chronic, and it is difficult for the
government to know what remedial steps are appropriate. Foreign
competition often is blamed for domestic economic problems. (In the
current cycle, until recently, we blamed the Japanese for their "unfair"
practices in virtually every business from automobiles to computer
chips.) As domestic economic woes intensify, there often is a trend
toward increased trade protectionism and tariff legislation. Whether
this takes the form of congressional action (as it usually does) or per-
mitting U.S. dollar debasement (this would mean that foreign goods
could not compete so effectively), protectionism occurs on various
levels. In the past this period has also witnessed consumer boycotts of
foreign goods.

Various attempts are made to regulate money supply, interest rates,
domestic spending and the tax structure. The net effect is a move
toward conservatism. Frequently, social trends also change dramatically. In the 1980s we saw a clear shift in attitudes, mores and behavior. It
becomes increasingly difficult for labor to triumph over business.
Business can no longer afford to pay the price as profits begin to
diminish partially as a result of the seemingly excessive demands of
labor. Strikes are longer lasting and more violent, and concessions to
labor slowly but surely diminish. During Stage 6, conservatism is often
on the increase.

Usually after several years of the initial decline, disinflation tends to
abate and the recovery period begins. Rather than respond to the
recovery by breathing a sigh of relief and claiming that the worst is

over, the intelligent investor should use the recovery period as an opportunity to further reduce debt, while moving into disinflation-type investments.

Stages 7 to 9

The precise duration for Stages 7 to 9 is difficult to predict since government action, or lack thereof, can significantly impact their time span. Typically, however, these are the worst years of the long wave: years during which substantial economic contraction, panics and repudiation of debt are not uncommon. Low debt, a high cash position and disinflation-type investments are favored during this period.

Stage 7: Gradual decline and start of secondary depression. Following the recovery period and unsuccessful tests of the economic peaks of previous economic cycles, the economy usually slides into a period of decline, disinflation and eventual depression. This is the most difficult time for the economy, the public, the government and individual markets. At first, prices drop slowly. Demand declines, wages decline, unemployment increases, bankruptcies increase, banks fail and interest rates decline persistently. Commodity prices fall across a broad front. Farmers suffer as prices for their goods drop almost without hiatus.

The decline can erase as much as 80 percent of the previous long-wave gains. Figures 5.7 through 5.11 show Stage 7 declines in various markets. Take some time to study these charts. You will observe that the declines are persistent, severe and precipitous. Prices tend to lose from 75 to 80 percent of their value by the time Stage 7 has drawn to a close. It should be noted that not all individual markets respond in a similar fashion to the Stage 7 decline inasmuch as they are also influenced by their individual cyclical patterns.

Stage 8: Extended decline. After the secondary decline has taken hold, bringing persistent price deterioration in many markets, the magnitude of the down moves tends to slow but the declines often continue for a period of years. The precise duration of Stage 8 is not fixed. It can be fairly short (perhaps several years), or it can run for as long as 10 years. During this stage the economy tends to recover from the

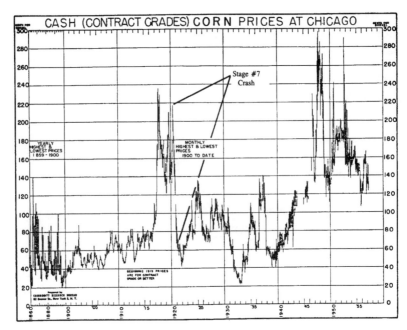

FIGURE 5.7 **Stage 7 Decline in Cash Corn (Reprinted with permission of Commodity Research Bureau)**

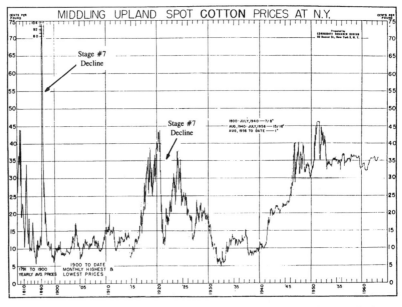

FIGURE 5.8 **Stage 7 Decline in Cash Cotton (Reprinted with permission of Commodity Research Bureau)**

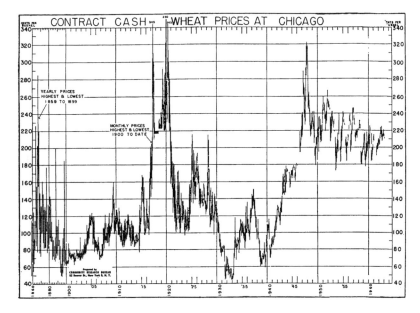

FIGURE 5·9   Stage 7 Decline in Cash Wheat (Reprinted with permission of Commodity Research Bureau)

panics, bankruptcies and severe economic contraction that characterized the previous phase. In fact, Stage 8 is actually a continuation of Stage 7. The only perceptible difference is that the decline tends to slow, and that recoveries typically are shorter. Some market analysts consider Stages 7 to 9 as essentially one stage.

Social attitudes, opinions and behavior during this stage continue to reflect increased conservatism. Religious practice is likely to be on the upswing. There is a "return to basics" attitude throughout the country, as people are forced to adjust to a simpler lifestyle, one uncomplicated by the availability of surplus capital or extravagant needs.

Political struggles continue as efforts are made to solve the problems of recession, disinflation and/or depression. There is a tendency for isolationism to increase. This trend will eventually lead the country into a war (known for the purposes of this analysis as the "bottom war"). It can be reasonably assumed that the Gulf War was the bottom war of the present cycle and that an economic low was seen at that time.

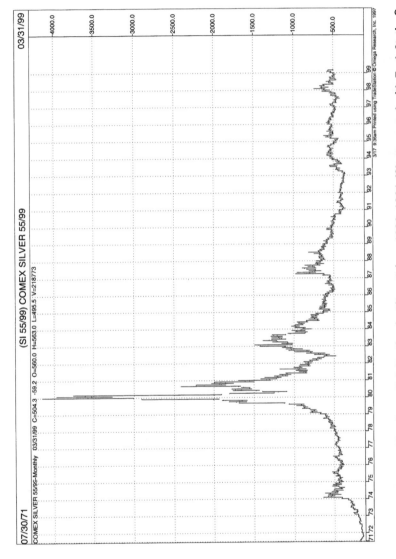

FIGURE 5.10 The Stage 7–8 Decline in Silver Prices 1980–1991 (Chart created with TradeStation® 2000; by Omega Research, Inc.) ©1997 Omega Research, Inc.

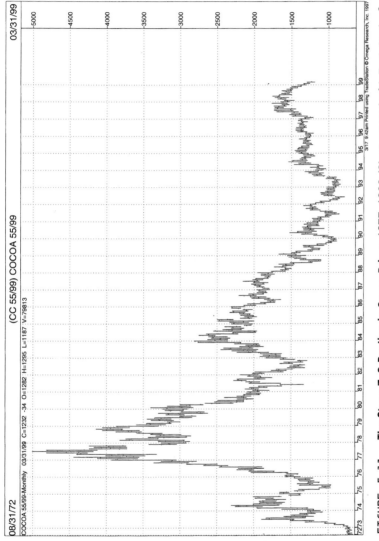

FIGURE 5.11 The Stage 7–8 Decline in Cocoa Prices 1977–1992 (Chart created with TradeStation® 2000; by Omega Research, Inc.) ©1997 Omega Research, Inc.

Virtually all prices continue on the downswing during Stage 8. Interest rates continue to decline. Money is no longer in great demand, since expansion is no longer a source of demand. Few individuals or firms are willing to go into debt, inasmuch as the perceived incentive to do so is minimal. Few industries flourish and many businesses fail. Eventually, the dark days of this stage bring with them increased conflict—at times domestic, more often international.

One interesting aspect of Stage 8 is the fact that technological discoveries made during this period are often those that help fuel the next long-wave upswing. During the most recent economic low, the technology for Internet communications, genetic engineering and electric fuel cells (to name just a few) were developed. Both the Internet and genetic engineering stocks have been leaders of the 1990s bull market in stocks.

Stage 9: Base building. The last stage of the long-wave cycle has its unique characteristics as well. Though it is commonly believed that prices at the end of the long-wave cycle stagnate, moving sideways for many years, this is not necessarily the case. Figures 5.12 through 5.14 show a number of different markets, focusing on Stage 9. Note that I have drawn a horizontal line below the Stage 9 base-building period.

As previously indicated, Stage 9 has frequently ended with a war. It is both functional and symbolic that the final and lowest stage of the long-wave cycle should end with a war: functional since it stimulates the economy, symbolic in its destruction of the "old" order. The Revolutionary War ended the long-wave cycle that bottomed in the 1780s. The Mexican-American War came near the economic lows of 1843. The Spanish-American War came with the economic lows of 1896, and World War II came near the economic lows of the late 1930s.

Typically, bottom wars have been popular wars, supported by the American public, whereas the top wars have not had a great deal of public support. Top wars are seen as ending prosperity, whereas bottom wars are seen as ending depression or recession. Bottom wars have come as a relief to the long period of depression or disinflation that preceded them.

Following the bottom war, there is a return to Stage 1. As in every one of the stages outlined in the preceding pages, there are no rigid start and/or end dates. At times the transition from one stage to another is rapid and easily discernible; at other times it is gradual and virtu-

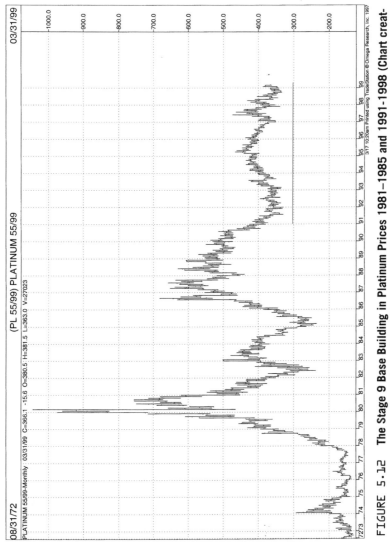

FIGURE 5.12 The Stage 9 Base Building in Platinum Prices 1981–1985 and 1991-1998 (Chart created with TradeStation® 2000; by Omega Research, Inc.) ©1997 Omega Research, Inc.

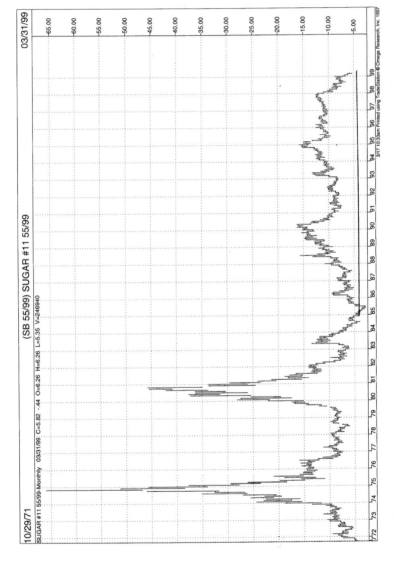

FIGURE 5.13   Stage 9 Base Building in Sugar Prices   (Chart created with TradeStation® 2000; by Omega Research, Inc.) ©1997 Omega Research, Inc.

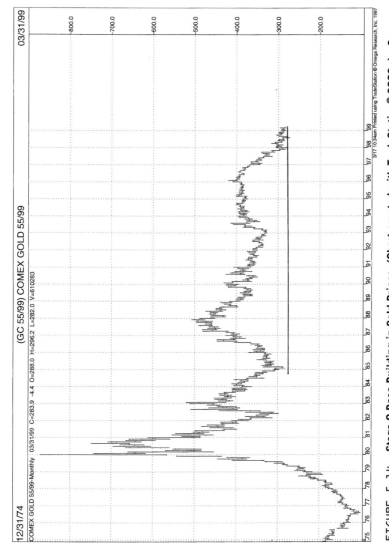

FIGURE 5.14 Stage 9 Base Building in Gold Prices (Chart created with TradeStation® 2000; by Omega Research, Inc.) ©1997 Omega Research, Inc.

ally imperceptible. I caution you not to form rigid generalizations about any of the stages. Every cycle is different, though they tend to follow the same basic patterns. Every cycle in every market is different from every previous cycle; however, there are sufficient similarities to allow forecasts, reasonable generalizations, and, most important, long-range investment planning.

Those who make an effort to examine current trends and economic events in the light of historical trends and economic realities are those who will benefit from the application of long-wave economic theory. Although the controversy about whether long-wave economic cycles exist will continue indefinitely, those who employ long-wave theory in making important economic decisions are convinced that the long-wave cycles are real.

Current Position of the Long-Wave Cycle

There has been much controversy about the long-wave economic cycles. While some observers and economists strongly assert that the cycles are major forces in economic trends, others claim that there is no proof to support their existence. Similarly, it is often argued that there are no phases or stages in markets or in economic trends. Obviously, I am one of those who not only claims these patterns exist, but who also feels that knowledge of their existence and characteristics can be a valuable tool for investment planning and asset protection. With this in mind, I offer the following observations as to where the U.S. economy and stock market currently stand in terms of both the long-wave cycle and its stages.

- Long-Wave Cyclical Low: I believe that the long-wave economic cycle has made its low. The low was likely made in the late 1980s and correlates closely with the Gulf War, which was most likely the "bottom war" of the long-term economic cycle. The strong behavior of stock prices as well as solid (noninflationary) growth suggest that my conclusion is correct.

- Accordingly, the U.S. economy is still in the early stages of a major growth cycle that is likely to continue until well into the 2010 time frame. The massive rally in stock prices could indicate that the growth portion of this economic up wave has contracted and that the next peak will be reached sooner in the cycle rather than at its midpoint.

- Long-term interest rates are bottoming based on their cyclical patterns. As they bottom and begin to climb there will be more "push–pull" in the U.S. economy. However, if rates climb at a relatively slow pace, there will be no lengthy declines in the stock market. Should Federal Reserve policy become aggressive in "combating" inflation, then several stock market declines could develop. At this time there are strong indications that commodity prices are bottoming. And this could well be the initial stimulus of an inflationary trend.

- Following a possibly severe decline in stocks due to the confluence of numerous fundamental and cyclical factors, the U.S. stock market is likely to resume its strong upward trend. A severe Y2K decline will likely present a buying opportunity; however, it may take several years for the market to recover from the selling panic. The astute investor will be prepared for Y2K by having sufficient buying power in the form of available investment capital.

Summary

The strong upward course of stock prices since the late 1980s suggests that the initial phases of a new economic cycle is being completed. Following a significant retracement, most likely resulting from Y2K and a variety of associated fundamental factors, the economy and the U.S. stock market will be ready to resume their upward course. I do not believe that Y2K will represent the end of an economic trend but rather a stumbling block on the road to higher levels.

CHAPTER
SIX

THE CRASH
AND THE GREATER FOOL

As you know, the rise in U.S. stock prices has been dramatic, lengthy and persistent. The long-range and short-range expectations of virtually all analysts and prognosticators have been surpassed significantly. A number of well-known and respected prognosticators have repeatedly claimed that the end of the bull market has come. To date, they have been totally wrong, time and time again. Eventually, they will be correct, but they will suffer immensely first. We do not want to become like them.

> To acquire wealth is not easy, yet to keep it is even more difficult. . . . It is said that wealth is like a viper which is harmless if a man knows how to take hold of it; but if he does not, it will twine around his head and bite him.
> —Frank K. Houston

The substantive issue is not when the top will occur or *if* the top will occur. We know for a fact that *there will be a top*. We also know from the history of the markets that the top will catch many people with too much stock, at prices that are too high. This will, of course, set the stage for the next bear market, and possibly for a severe chain reaction of economic catastrophes. If there are only limited negative consequences from Y2K problems, then we will all breathe a major sigh of relief. However, if there is a severe economic cataclysm due to Y2K effects, then preparation will be your strongest asset.

One serious problem that has been developing for some time now is what I call, for lack of a better term, "Artificial Wealth."

The "Greater Fool Theory" and Y2K

A simple way to understand the developing situation is to realize that, in many respects, the U.S. stock market is based on what has appropriately been called "The Greater Fool Theory."

As you read this book, stock markets throughout the world may still be moving strongly higher or they may be declining. Regardless of their direction, the fact is that the major bull market from the 1980s until at least 1999 has been the biggest and most persistent bull market ever. It has taken many stocks to their highest prices in history regardless of their real value. Investors, in their need to participate in the game and profit from it, have paid higher and higher prices for worthless stocks. They have done so in the hope that what they bought at $40 per share might be at $60 per share in several months, or perhaps even at $100 per share in a year. They bought their shares from someone who had earlier bought the stock at $25 per share and sold it at $40 per share in the belief that the price had reached its peak or close to it. And if the buyer at $40 per share is successful in selling at $60 per share, then the buyer at $60 will be hoping to sell at a higher price still. This is the "buy high/sell higher" school of thought.

The intent is clear and it is standard procedure in a capitalist society. It is, in fact, the crux of what we call investing. Investing in and of itself is reasonable and built on a solid foundation, if what we invest in has solid backing behind it. At times, however, the selling price of a home or a piece of land or a stock or a commodity reaches levels that are not truly representative of the underlying worth of the item. We have seen many periods in history that have witnessed the rapid speculative appreciation of prices to levels that are entirely out of phase with reality. The Dutch Tulip Mania and the South Sea Company Bubble are just two such instances. In each case, the price of a virtually worthless item was bid to higher and higher levels as speculators bought with the intention of selling at a profit to a "greater fool."

This is the "Greater Fool Theory" of markets: Most sellers believe that they have milked their investment for as much as they could get under the circumstances (unless they were forced to sell), and they often consider the buyer to be a greater fool than they themselves have been. The entire cycle of buying or selling in a speculative market accelerates to a point of insanity and only ends when the last fool has paid the highest price. Soon, the ultimate fool will be forced to sell his or her holdings to an even greater fool but at a lower price. The new fool will then be forced to sell at a loss to yet another losing fool. And so the story goes.

The biggest bull market in history has produced an army of fools. Many have profited, but there will be many who will be left holding the bag when the top comes. (The top may already have come by the time you read these words.)

What will be especially distressing this time is that the Y2K crisis may exacerbate the situation. When and if the Y2K crisis reaches its full intensity, it may be difficult for investors to sell their shares at any price simply because the order processing system at their brokerage house may not work. Or, if they're dealing on line, they may have even worse problems. The resulting panic will inspire a massive rush of selling. Prices will likely plunge so fast that the already taxed electronic systems will be unable to keep track of transactions. This will cause many more investors to panic and sell. And this will cause a chain reaction of lower prices in many stocks. Those stocks that have risen on pure speculation will fall the most. They could easily lose 50 percent of their value or more overnight.

Paper Millionaires

In 1998, one of the cable news networks featured a most significant and disturbing story. The report was entitled "The New Millionaires." It presented some interesting and potentially frightening facts about what the big bull market in stocks has done to the pocketbooks of many retirees who own stock pension plans. Many of these individuals have been accumulating stock for 25 to 30 years as part of their company pension and/or retirement plans. Stock that they have accumulated, for example, at an average cost of perhaps $25 per share may now be valued at $140 per share.

The end result is that they're millionaires—at least on paper. They have considerable *unrealized* wealth. The program went on to report that in one Wisconsin town alone, a town that is home to a large consumer products company, in the last few years the number of paper millionaires has increased to several thousand! You may ask, "So, what's wrong with that?"

Consider this: Let's assume that while most of the new paper millionaires are reasonable and conservative people, there are others who may be taking their paper wealth seriously, accumulating large credit card and installment debt expecting a continued rise in their paper assets. What would happen if the stock market suffers a serious correction? In a matter of weeks, a good 35 percent of their wealth may disappear. Their accumulated debt could become a burden that might force them into bankruptcy. What could be worse is the possible chain reaction this forced stock and asset liquidation could create.

This decline could well be precipitated by a series of severe problems arising from the MB situation. The closing of several banks that cannot access their records or run their financial software could well cause a domino effect creating panic among investors who are afraid that their banks will fail. The panic could easily spread to the stock market, resulting in an avalanche of selling. Those who are unprepared will see their paper millions turn into nothing within a matter of hours at the worst or within a few weeks at best.

In the early 1980s when land and real estate prices were at record highs, there were hundreds of farmers who were paper millionaires by virtue of the fact that they had thousands of acres of farmland then valued at $7000 per acre or more. Over the course of several years they sat and watched their land values plummet to $2500 an acre as prices spiraled lower and lower. Many were unwilling to sell; others were forced to sell since they had borrowed against their paper profits. While this situation developed in the relatively slow-moving land market, it is typical of how markets and investors behave when prices decline.

The worst part of this scenario is that many of today's paper millionaires are inexperienced or unsophisticated investors. They have acquired their wealth not by careful analysis of stock trends and fundamentals but rather through the accumulation of shares at a low average price in pension and retirement funds. Still other investors who have done well have never had to live through lengthy bear markets. They are totally unfamiliar with declining trends and their characteristics. They fail to realize that bear markets fall faster than bull markets rise. They do not understand that a stock that has gone up from $14 per share to $73 per share over a period of three years can decline from $73 per share to $25 per share in a matter of weeks or even days.

In a very real sense, the big bull market that began in the 1980s and continued through the 1990s is built on air, on expectations of earnings, on anticipated profits and on forecasts. It is a known fact of market history and market life that such inflated markets and prices tend to deflate quickly. It takes great effort to blow up a balloon. Yet the balloon can deflate in a matter of several seconds. The real danger of a market panic inspired by Y2K is that it will spread like wildfire through an artificially inflated market, and this will result in a chain reaction of selling, the likes of which have not been seen since the Crash of 1929 or the Crash of 1987.

Artificial Money

We have all been trained to think that the key force in terms of money supply expansion and contraction is the Federal Reserve. This may not be true. While the Fed can expand or contract the supply of money by starting or stopping the printing presses, the stock and commodity markets can do so as well. The only difference is that stock and commodity market trends are not *directly* under government control.

While a strong stock market means a potentially strong economy, a stock market that has risen as much as the current U.S. market has done poses a serious danger since it creates artificial money by valuing stocks higher and higher. The money it creates stands for nothing more than the liquidation value of the shares (i.e., corporate assets), and what people are willing to pay for the stock.

Consider the company that wants to raise cash for expansion. It has several choices. It could go to a bank and borrow the money. It could issue corporate bonds or it could issue new stock. In effect, issuing new stock is a way of raising millions of dollars at virtually no cost to the company. By issuing 2 million shares of stock at, let's say, $15 per share, it can raise $30 million quickly. (Of course, new stock offerings have to be approved by the Securities and Exchange Commission.) Every new stock offering sucks money away from banks and savings and into the less secure stock market. The end result is a market that is not built on a firm foundation. Artificial money created by this kind of market can disappear in a matter of days, and it will!

The Bottom Line

Here are my thoughts about a reversal in the U.S. stock market trend in conjunction with and in reaction to a variety of Y2K problems. (Note that this does *not* imply that the market panic will begin from a new all-time high in the stock market. The market may already have peaked when the panic hits.)

POSSIBLE SCENARIOS

My analysis here is not intended to be a stock market forecast. Rather it is intended to provide you with possible scenarios of what may come so that you can get a lead on the market and the panic as well. (If you have followed my suggestions, you will have taken action well before any problems begin or, at the worst, when problems first arise.)

1. *A downturn in the stock market will likely be one of the first effects of a Y2K crisis.* The stock market is highly sensitive to the kinds of disruptions that may occur when and if the millennium madness becomes pandemic. If the market is strong and moving higher when the Y2K problems begin, then the market could easily use Y2K as an "excuse" for making a major top. In other words, Y2K could be the precipitating event that appears to "cause" the top. Remember, however, that Y2K will not be the true cause of a top or of a sustained decline.

2. *The biggest bull market in history will not end with a whimper.* It will likely end with a new all-time high on record-high volume. This type of peak is known as a "blowoff top." (As of this writing the blowoff has not yet happened.)

In 1998 and early 1999, New York Stock Exchange volume had been running from about 350 million to about 600 million shares daily. A blowoff top day or series of days should be accompanied by record-high volume as well as a record-high price range (that is, the spread between the high and the low of the day will be at its greatest point). The Dow Jones Industrials, for example, could have a very large trading range, perhaps 600 points or more from low to high, on such a day (or on several days).

3. *The "blowoff top" could come on the heels of very positive news* prior to a wave of negative news, most likely due to Y2K-related break-

downs or disruptions. The bullish news might be a drop in interest rates, unexpectedly bullish corporate earnings reports or a very constructive political development. The bearish news could be a run on banks, the shutdown of an automobile production plant or an announcement that Social Security checks will not be available for several months.

4. *Prior to the peak there will be numerous warning signs.* Among these will be rampant speculation in essentially worthless stocks, a wave of new public offerings, tales of soaring prices in new issues on their first trading day, stories of vast fortunes made by new and/or relatively inexperienced traders, and more. In addition to these danger signs, positive news about the market will appear to have little impact on prices. The market will appear hesitant. What may seem like good news to the market will likely have limited or minimal upside effect on prices while trading volume continues to be heavy, and the world will wonder why the news can't spur the market higher. Optimism will have limited effect in moving prices higher.

5. *Trading in Standard and Poor's, NASDAQ and Dow Jones futures and options, as well as trading in OEX options, may become highly illiquid.* Floor brokers may refuse orders or refuse to accept anything but "at the market" orders. Price executions will be terrible as a result of poor liquidity. (Disruptions in electronic trading may be among the first warning signs that a Y2K problem is developing.) The inability of pit brokers to be certain about the accuracy of the orders they are receiving or the ability of recordkeeping systems to accurately monitor their positions, price quotations and news will prove problemmatic and may sharply curtail or halt trading.

6. *How minor Y2K-related problems, if any, affect the stock market initially will be an indicator of its possible reaction to more severe problems.* If the experts are to be believed, then some problems could crop up by mid 1999. Remember that the problems themselves may not be nearly so important as trader, money manager and investor reaction to the problems. This will be your *most important* barometer. The trading public has the ability to send world markets crashing if they panic. As I have pointed out, we have more to fear from public reaction to Y2K problems than we do from Y2K problems themselves. The likelihood of panic is worse than the likelihood of problems. Problems can be solved, but panic has its own agenda and is difficult to control once it starts.

7. *How markets behave after their initial reaction to Y2K problems is another very important sign.* Say, for example, that stocks sell off sharply following an announcement by the Social Security system that they will "shut down" for 10 days to repair unexpected "problems" with their computer systems. If the market ignores the news, then you have an indication of what investors and professional traders consider important or unimportant in its potential to hurt the economy or corporate profits. If, however, the markets decline sharply and *do not recover* quickly, then there will be more severe problems. In this case the market is telling you what to expect and you had better heed the warning.

8. *The behavior of foreign markets to Y2K problems is another key indicator.* In particular, watch markets in Asia and South America where Y2K readiness may not be at so high a level as in the United States. Remember that we live in a global economic community, and a domino effect of declines is a real possibility. We have seen it happen before and we will see it happen again. We are *not immune* to the effects of problems in other countries.

9. *Expect government policy to be positive and confident.* This is what government should do in a time of crisis. But no matter what they say, watch carefully what they do. If, for example, a "bank holiday" is declared, then you will know that problems are severe. Don't be surprised to see the President of the United States address the nation in a special television broadcast if Y2K problems become particularly disruptive and serious.

PRECAUTIONS YOU CAN TAKE TO AVOID PROBLEMS

A market top or severe decline is highly likely if Y2K problems and/or investor panic develop. Given these concerns, I recommend the following precautions:

- *Watch for warning signs.* Although we cannot anticipate the exact timing of a top, you now know some of the warning signs. Should these develop, the most rational and conservative action is to *either exit stocks in advance* or *decide, in advance, not to panic.* The savvy investor may, in fact, seize the opportunity to establish short positions and/or to speculate on the buy side when and if prices fall sharply.

▪ *If you are long on stocks, use trailing stop losses* and/or any other form of protection to lock in a certain percentage of your profit while still giving your positions plenty of room to move higher.

▪ *Avoid, or at the first signs of danger, liquidate positions in futures options, OEX options and stock options.* In the event of a blowoff and reversal down, these vehicles will probably become illiquid and, hence, not tradable.

▪ *Be on the short side or, at least, avoid being caught on the long side.* Remember that a 10 percent market correction with the Dow Industrials at 2500 (in 1990) would be 250 points. With the Dow at 10,000, a 10 percent correction would be 1000 points. At a 20 percent Dow correction from 10,000, the decline would be over 2000 points! The stock market crash of 1987 witnessed a drop from about 2650 to a low of 1707. That was a correction of about 30 percent. A 30 percent correction of the Dow at 10,000 would be 3000 points—and it could happen in a matter of days. Clearly this would be the biggest point crash in U.S. stock market history. Declines such as these seem to come out of "nowhere," but if you're watching the signs and symptoms then you'll know ahead of time when things are turning stale.

▪ *Act well in advance.* While the well-capitalized investor and nimble fund manager may be fast enough to take profits before the bulk of the crash has started, the smaller investor could easily be caught in the avalanche of selling. If market history repeats, then the smaller investor will take the biggest beating. If, however, we take the position that the biggest players in this market are institutional, then there is no doubt in my mind that several institutions will be destroyed by the tsunami that may develop. Don't wait to see what will happen. This would be like lighting a fuse on a stick of dynamite and waiting to see if the fuse will work. The risk is much too high.

I'm concerned about the possible chain reaction of events that may follow either a blowoff top in the stock market and/or a Y2K crisis. This includes safety of monies invested in mutual funds as well as bank accounts. Take the necessary steps to protect yourself here as well. Remember that selling out your holdings and getting back in again might cost you some commissions as well as some loss in potential profits; however, insurance costs money. It is part of a rational and effective strategy.

Remember, if your funds are invested in crisis-related vehicles (for example, gold, Treasury bills or bonds, and the like) you will have some degree of protection. Such a strategy could actually make you money as your strategic investments rise in value as millions clamor to get in at the last moment.

Summary

Stock markets the world over are highly sensitive and reactive to domestic and international events that may, in the eyes of investors and traders, impact corporate profits or economic stability. At times investor panic and declines in stocks are used by professional traders as opportunities to buy. At times, however, investor panic can lead to a chain reaction of selling that accelerates and soon engulfs the market resulting in massive liquidation across a broad base of stocks. Y2K problems may cause such an avalanche of panic liquidation. Whether this selling is sensible is not at issue. Panic is an extreme reaction that is rarely effective and most often counterproductive, nevertheless it does occur and the intelligent investor must be prepared for it.

FIRST LINE OF DEFENSE:
PRECIOUS METALS

As you may know, the precious metals markets are favored investments under very specific conditions. First, they tend to be attractive when there is strong inflation. Second, they tend to be a safe haven during times of economic turmoil

> Fear is like fire: If controlled, it will help you; if uncontrolled, it will rise up and destroy you. Men's actions depend to a great extent upon fear. We do things either because we enjoy doing them or because we are afraid not to do them. This sort of fear has no relation to physical or moral courage. It is inspired by the knowledge that we are not adequately prepared to face the future and the events it may bring—poverty perhaps, or injury or death.
> —John F. Milburn

or uncertainty. These have been the two traditionally favored times in which gold, silver, platinum and palladium have been aggressively bought by investors and speculators. Those of you who have been watching the precious metals markets know that gold prices have declined persistently since the early 1980s. There have been only minor upmoves since, and they have not lasted long. Why? There are several reasons:

- Although there has been political and economic uncertainty, there have also been solutions to problems. Even issues such as the U.S. budget deficit, bank failures and Middle East conflicts have been effectively resolved. Even the Gulf War was resolved favorably. As a result, investors have not flocked into precious metals since there was no need to run for cover.

▪ The U.S. stock market has been rising persistently. With the exception of a major corrective decline in 1987, the course has been a strong and steady one. Hence, there has been no need for investors to own precious metals.

▪ Supplies of precious metals (with the exception of palladium) have been plentiful and demand has not, as a result, been a factor in keeping prices high.

▪ There has been virtually no inflation in most American and European economies; therefore, there has been no need for investors to get into precious metals as a means of protecting their assets from the effects of inflation.

The coming Y2K problems, or their aftermath, could very well change this. If serious problems develop in the international financial community or in stock markets as a result of Y2K computer problems, investors may flock into gold. (My long-term studies on gold prices suggest that this may be one of the best ways to protect yourself against the uncertainties of what may develop during the coming MC.)

What's more, I believe precious metals will rise again, and that rise will begin well before the start of millennium problems. The rise may be limited in time and magnitude or it may prove to be a lengthy one with considerable magnitude. How the precious metals behave will be a function of which of several scenarios play out.

When the MC is upon us there will be few markets that will appreciate in value initially. The key direction of markets will be bearish. Moves up will be relatively brief, but potentially violent. Moves down will be severe and extended. One of the few safe havens will likely be the precious metals markets. While they may not necessarily rise in value, the odds are that they will retain their value relative to other markets.

In other words, while the stock market may decline 35 percent (or much more), gold and precious metals will likely not decline much, if at all. They may, in fact, rise. The degree of rally potential is an intangible that will need to be evaluated when the occasion arises and within the context of several possible MC scenarios. There will be many variables to factor into that equation.

Since buying and selling precious metals in their various forms is not something to be plunged into blindly, in this chapter I will let you know what you may expect and how you can protect yourself in the event of a serious economic catastrophe resulting from the coming Y2K problems.

Emotional Extremes

Few investment opportunities stimulate either as much interest or as much emotion as metals and precious metals. Whether precious metals, industrial metals or strategic metals, investors and speculators have had a long-standing love/hate relationship with these markets. In particular, the quest to own and/or control precious metals has, for literally thousands of years, driven speculators to risk their fortunes, soldiers to risk their lives and leaders to risk their power. Since the early 1980s, gold, silver and platinum have failed to attract much interest; however, I believe that this is about to change (if it has not already happened by the time you read this book).

Bridge Over Troubled Y2K Waters

Precious metals have always been considered a safe haven during times of turmoil, whether political, economic or monetary. In fact, the right to own, trade, speculate and invest in precious metals has acquired the status of an inalienable, or even God-given, right. While we have come a long way from the arcane and mystical teachings of alchemists, our continued fascination with metals, particularly the precious kind, has grown steadily. Stocks may come and go, bonds eventually mature and businesses may flourish and dissolve, but precious metals endure.

Since the early 1980s, the role of gold and silver as protection against uncertainty or upheaval has been diminished as prices have declined steadily. Yet, as silver and gold have declined, palladium prices have exploded and platinum has increased in value. (The fundamental reasons behind the spectacular rise in palladium prices relate specifically to production problems and the disruption of supplies in the production areas of former Soviet states.)

If you're preparing to invest in the metals markets, some questions will arise that need to be addressed:

- Why do metals elicit such strong emotions among investors and speculators?
- What makes them so attractive?
- What is the long-term investment potential of the metals markets?
- What are the premier metal investments of today? And which metals are likely to attract a future following?
- How will metals fare during the coming Millennium Crash?
- Why should the average investor be interested in metals?
- Why be interested in an investment that has such a volatile, and at times violent, history?
- Why take the time to learn about strategic metals, a seemingly esoteric subject?

I suggest that you keep some of these questions in mind as you read the pages that follow. In the end, you will be convinced, as I am, that the future is likely to be bright for all three of the metals groups, particularly if and when the Millennium Crash becomes a reality. You will see that your own future could be even brighter if you can use your knowledge of metals in a comprehensive program of investment and/or speculation.

In fact, your financial survival during the coming difficult times may very well depend on what you do in the metals markets and how you do it. This is not to say that the only reasonable hedge against the coming crisis will be in the metals markets. However, I must advise you that a position in the metals markets will constitute an important aspect of your protective portfolio.

Figures 7.1 and 7.2 show the price history of silver and gold in the United States. Note that since gold ownership was legalized in the United States in the 1970s, the price history in Figure 7.1 prior to 1972 reflects an index of gold stock prices.

Now let's take a brief look at these markets to see if we can glean any useful information about them in light of their long-term histories.

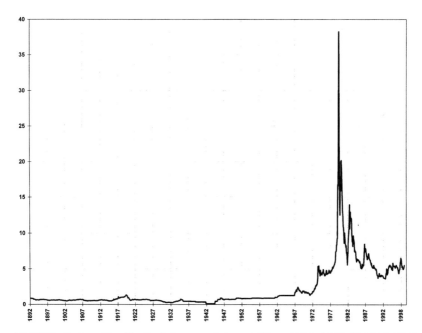

FIGURE 7.1   Monthly Cash Average Price of Silver 1892–1999 (©1998 MBH Commodity Advisors Inc.)

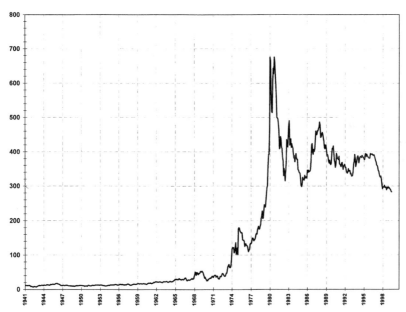

FIGURE 7.2   Monthly U.S. Average Gold Index and Gold 1941–1999 (©1998 MBH Commodity Advisors Inc.)

GOLD

The time period from 1971 to the early 1980s witnessed a long and exceptionally large move up in gold prices. The top was followed by an initial decline, which was then followed by a move back to the all-time high. Thereafter the market fell sharply. Although there were several intervening up moves, the major trend has been down. Gold has lost about half its value from the 1976 low to the 1982 top. An interesting correlation can be drawn between gold prices and the stock market. Figure 7.3 shows this relationship. Some analysts claim that gold and the stock market tend to move in opposite directions. They believe that when the stock market is declining, gold prices are rallying (or should rally). As you can see from this chart, this conclusion is not always true.

In recent years, however (i.e., since 1988), this has, in fact, been the case. As Figure 7.3 shows, the U.S. stock market and gold prices have been moving in opposite directions. What can we conclude from this relationship? I suspect that if and when the stock market begins a severe decline, gold prices could very well begin a strong rally. Figure 7.3 shows this relationship on a monthly basis while Figure 7.4 shows the same relationship from 1996 to 1999 on a weekly basis. Note the opposite trends. It is reasonable to conclude that if and when the Y2K crisis spills over into world stock markets, gold will be a safe haven. (You will find a strategic plan for accumulating gold and gold shares in a later chapter.)

SILVER

Silver is not essentially a precious metal. It is mainly used for industrial applications. However, it tends to move with gold in times of crisis. Its appeal is primarily for the smaller trader although this is not always the case. Figure 7.5 shows the relationship between silver prices and S&P from 1988 to 1999. Although there have been times when silver and S&P prices moved in relative tandem, this has not been the case since 1988. Interestingly enough, silver held its value better than gold during the recent major bull market in stocks. It is likely that when and if stock prices begin a severe decline in response to Y2K problems and panics, silver prices will rise, at least in sympathy with gold. Figure 7.6 shows the weekly relationship between silver prices and the S&P 500

FIGURE 7·3   The Relationship Between Gold (top) and S&P 500 (bottom) on a Monthly Basis from 1988 to 1999 (Copyright 1999 CQG, Inc.)

FIGURE 7·4   The Relationship Between Gold (top) and S&P 500 (bottom) on a Weekly Basis from Late 1996 to 1999 (Copyright 1999 CQG, Inc.)

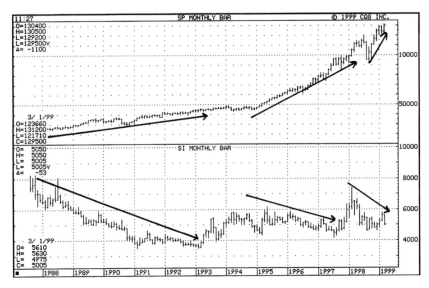

FIGURE 7.5 Cash S&P 500 Monthly (top) and Silver Prices (bottom) 1988–1999 (Copyright 1999 CQG, Inc.)

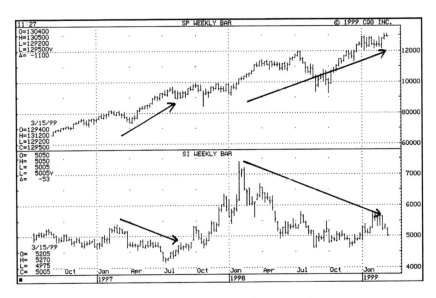

FIGURE 7.6 Cash S&P 500 Weekly (top) and Silver Prices (bottom) 1996–1999 (Copyright 1999 CQG, Inc.)

from late 1996 through 1999. The divergent relationship here is not nearly so pronounced as it has been between gold prices and the stock market.

PLATINUM

This market is not actively traded; however, it has made some large moves since the 1960s. Given the fact that platinum has very specific fundamentals related to production in the former Soviet states and Africa, the market tends to rise and fall independently of trends in the U.S. stock market. There has been an important historical ratio relationship between platinum and gold. Platinum prices and the stock market have also shown an inverse relationship. Figure 7.7 shows the trends in platinum and the S&P 500 on a monthly basis since 1988. As you can see, there has been an inverse relationship between platinum prices and stock index prices.

FIGURE 7.7   Cash S&P 500 Monthly (top) and Platinum Prices (bottom) 1988–1999 (Copyright 1999 CQG, Inc.)

Bullion Coins

There are many different types of bullion coins to choose from. Although they are all similar in terms of metal content, the differences among them are essentially aesthetic and price related. Coins such as South African Krugerrands, Canadian Maple Leafs and Chinese Pandas are popular among collectors, but the primary reason for owning bullion coins is for their bullion value. While you may see many advertisements touting the rarity of certain bullion coins, you must decide for yourself whether you are interested in numismatics or in bullion.

If you are indeed interested in bullion, then virtually any bullion coin will do the job. Since there are so many different gold, silver, palladium and platinum bullion coins, and since there are so many more coming to market every year, it would be useless to discuss with you the various types of bullion coins you could buy. By the time you read this, the information will be dated, but I will give you some guidelines on how to choose, purchase and store bullion coins.

GOLD AND SILVER BULLION COINS

These are among the most popular and plentiful of the bullion coins. Remember that when you buy these, you will be paying for the metal content and broker commission as well as sales tax, in some cases. You are advised, therefore, to shop around and compare prices before you buy, since commissions vary considerably. Also make certain that you are dealing with a reputable coin dealer. Be sure that you take possession of the coins you are buying. Through the years many investors have been cheated by various schemes, all of which have involved delayed delivery to the buyer, "holding" the coins for the customer, or both.

Another factor to consider in buying gold bullion coins is liquidity. Eventually there will come a time for you to sell your coins. You must be prepared to sell quickly, since market tops develop rapidly and since there can be substantial price swings when a top is reached. You should, therefore, accumulate the most popular issues, since these will be the ones in greatest demand when the top is at hand.

It has been my experience that prices from one dealer to another can vary considerably during the time of a market top. I urge you to compare prices when selling. You'll be surprised at the different prices you'll be quoted, and at the different prices you'll get for different quantities of coins. You may be quoted a better price for a larger quantity.

Furthermore, I suggest that you do some research before selecting a coin dealer. There have been instances of forged bullion coins, so you are better off dealing with larger firms that will stand behind the authenticity of the coins they sell. Don't be afraid to ask questions about their policies. That's the only way you'll find out what you need to know.

In buying silver bullion coins, remember that you will need a much larger quantity of silver bullion, since the price of silver as compared to gold is considerably smaller. A bag of so-called junk silver, which consists of U.S. circulated silver coins, weighs about 45 pounds. For the same amount of money you can have about eight to ten one-troy-ounce gold coins.

PLATINUM AND PALLADIUM BULLION COINS

These coins are, in my opinion, the most interesting and often most attractive to collect, but they are considerably less liquid and, therefore, more difficult to sell. There are not many platinum coin issues and even fewer palladium issues. While you can accumulate these, you should make certain that there will be a dealer who will buy them back from you when the time comes. While prices could move dramatically higher, the lack of a liquid market will result in your not getting a good price when you want to sell. This is an important consideration if you plan to profit from your investment.

STORING BULLION COINS

If you plan to accumulate a sizable position in bullion coins, then you should be concerned about storage. While some investors choose to keep their coins at home, perhaps under the floorboards, in a mattress, in the freezer or buried in their backyard, there are other ways to store your coins. The most common way is to rent bank safe-deposit boxes and store your coins there until you are ready to sell. Since these coins can be quite heavy and can take a large amount of space (particularly silver), you will need considerable space for a large quantity of bullion.

I suggest that you keep boxes at a number of different banks. Through the years there has been much talk about the safety of items stored in bank safe-deposit boxes. Some feel that in the event of an emergency or banking crisis you may not be given access to your vault. If you are concerned about this, then I suggest you store your bullion coins in a private vault not run by a bank or other financial institution. There are many such firms throughout the country, particularly in larger urban centers.

WHEN TO BUY BULLION COINS

Since bullion coins must be purchased for 100 percent cash (that is, unlike stocks and futures, they cannot be bought on margin), you will want to accumulate your position over a period of time. The best way to do this is by dollar-cost averaging. In other words, make regular purchases over an extended period of time well before the bottom of the market has been reached. By buying at lower and lower prices you will slowly but surely bring your average cost down, and when the market begins its upswing, you will have accumulated a substantial position at a relatively low average cost.

Any of the following strategies will work:

1. Buy coins on a scale-down basis only. That means buy only if the price is lower this time than it was the last time you bought.
2. Buy bullion coins only when prices are below a predetermined level.
3. Buy bullion coins monthly or weekly, preferably on a scale-down basis.
4. Buy a larger quantity when prices are lower than they were the last time you bought. For example, let's assume you bought one gold bullion coin at $397 last month and that the price this month is $347. You might decide to buy two coins. You could also determine a scale for every $25 or $50 drop below your original purchase price.

HOW TO SHOP FOR THE BEST PRICE

While bullion coin prices are tied closely to the value of bullion, you'll be able to save money if you shop around for your coins. Not only will you find the lowest commissions, but you may also find lower base prices for the coins. I suggest that you have between four to six sources each month and that you contact them when you are ready to buy. Learn the price and then make your transactions.

Selling your coins, however, is a different matter. You will want to sell when prices are shooting ever higher. It is always easiest to sell on the way up, and it is always easiest to buy on the way down. If you check with your dealers several times a day when prices are rising sharply, you'll see that prices can vary considerably. Accept the fact that you're not going to get the very top of a move, nor will you get the very bottom of a move. Be prepared to sell out your holdings more quickly than you accumulated them. While market bottoms can take weeks, often months, to develop, market tops can happen in a matter of days. You will need to adjust your buying and selling strategies accordingly.

NUMISMATICS AND NUMISMATIC COIN FUNDS

While numismatic coins offer tremendous potential to the skilled and patient investor, it is a subject entirely unto itself. Some feel that this market offers the best of all worlds since it combines rarity with the value of bullion. A study of the performance history of numismatics confirms this opinion, but investing profitably in numismatic coins is not simple. I feel that all investors should own some numismatic coins, but the best way to do this is by enlisting the services of a professional dealer or expert unless, of course, you have the time and skill necessary to make informed decisions.

As an alternative to collecting rare coins, you may turn your capital over to professional managers who will buy coins for you. While the returns from some of these programs have been good, there are some things you should consider before you commit funds, such as commissions, management fees, experience of the managers, condition of the markets and the details of the programs themselves.

Here are some things to evaluate before putting your money with a professionally managed coin fund:

1. Are the commission charges reasonable?
2. What are the management fees and/or incentive fees? Are they reasonable?
3. What are the credentials of the program managers? Are they experienced numismatists?

4. Has the firm had previous coin programs and, if so, what have been the results?

5. Can you sell your interest at any time? If so, what are the details and charges? Are you locked in for a certain minimum length of time?

6. How are the coins acquired? Are they bought at auction, or are they bought from the affiliated companies of the firm or from its directors? It is preferable that they be bought from sources other than the firm's managers or affiliated companies, since this would create a conflict of interest.

7. How will the coins be sold? Will they be sold at auction or privately placed? Coins sold at auction usually get better prices.

8. Is there a loss-cutoff provision? In other words, will the program cease operations if net asset value drops below a given amount?

9. Are there any other provisions for the protection of the investors?

10. Is the fund registered properly with the appropriate state and/or federal agencies?

Consider these questions carefully, and before you take any action, consult with your attorney. Always ask for referrals from the firm, and don't do business with any individual or firm that you have not carefully checked first.

GUIDELINES FOR INVESTING IN COINS

Buying bullion coins is an excellent way to get started if you plan to invest in metals. Before investing in coins:

1. Locate several coin dealers in your area and check prices regularly. You will come to know whose prices are the best and whose commissions are the lowest.

2. Be sure to check the credentials of numismatists if you decide to enter this area of metals investing.

3. Before you send funds to anyone for any program, investment plan, coin or coin-related plan, check with your attorney or advisor.

4. When you buy coins, do so on a dollar-cost average basis. It is the most reasonable and sensible way of buying coins, and it will help you get the best average purchase price.

5. When you sell your bullion coins, be prepared to act much more quickly than when you bought the coins.

6. Remember that market peaks come quickly and that you will need to respond much more quickly than you did when you accumulated your position.

7. Don't forget that liquidity is very important. If you plan to accumulate a large position in bullion coins, then you must do so in coins that are easily liquidated.

8. You can often save money by shopping for the best prices and the best commissions. Don't be afraid to negotiate with dealers, particularly if you are buying or selling larger quantities or if you have been a good customer.

9. There is no need for you to pay a premium for special bullion-coin issues. If you want to collect coins, then do so as part of your numismatic portfolio; however, do not get this mixed up with your bullion-coin strategy.

10. Such things as medals, commemoratives, proof coin sets, special issue coins, etc., are all items that will require you to pay a premium, and often a healthy one. Do not confuse these with your bullion-coin purchase plan. Unless the market for these specialty items turns sharply higher, you will probably not recoup your original purchase price when you sell, particularly if you do not hold these items for a long time.

11. The bullion-coin strategy is a slow and steady one. You may accumulate coins for up to several years while watching your dollars return no profits, or even shrink. This is normal, since market bottoms take a long time to develop. But keep in mind that your plan is designed to take advantage of the up market that will surely follow.

12. There are many excellent coin dealers and coin advisory services that can be helpful as you make important investment decisions. Do a little research and find a service or advisor who can help you.

13. Don't forget that storage is a significant problem, particularly in silver bullion coins. Make arrangements for storage that is both safe and accessible.

14. When you see prices turn sharply higher, and when the situation appears to be incredibly positive, be prepared to liquidate some of your holdings, if not all of them, and be prepared to do so quickly.

Controlling Risk in the Metals Markets

Before buying any of the metals as a hedge against possible Y2K problems, you will need to understand the risks associated with precious
metals investments. I assume most of you are well aware of the potential risk that accompanies virtually all investments. The risks associated
with investments in metals are particularly large. Much of the risk in metals is based on the fact that the price of metals can gyrate wildly in emotional response to political and economic events worldwide. This will be
especially true when the millennium crisis hits in earnest. There's no
telling how volatile the markets will become. It is therefore imperative
to have well-established positions *before* the problems begin.

When emotional reactions are severe, so are risk and reward. What
exactly are the risks? Why are they especially large in the metals markets? What can be done to minimize risk? How can we recognize and
analyze risk?

INTERNATIONAL VOLATILITY

The metals markets that I recommend for inclusion in your Y2K
Survival Portfolio (silver, platinum and gold) have an international following. They are important barometers of economic activity, and they
are followed closely throughout the world by both investors and speculators. As a consequence, these and other metals are especially sensitive to virtually all types of economic and political events. At times
these events will have a major impact on prices, causing them to move
wildly; at other times the effects of international developments will be
minimal. I can't guarantee that these markets will move higher if and
when stocks the world over move lower; however, I believe that they
will offer protection and relative stability in an unstable environment.
The best-case scenario is, of course, that they will move substantially
higher.

In order for the metals to move higher in response to developments
in economies, politics or other markets, there must be a confluence of
patterns in all sectors. I believe the *confluence of changes* in cyclical
patterns for stocks, interest rates, commodity prices and the Y2K problems are combining to create an environment like those that have

caused precious metals to move higher in the past. This means, for example, that a terrorist attack in Jerusalem may *not* result in a rise in gold prices if the major pattern of gold prices is downward. In that event, the rise in the price of gold in response to the terrorist act might be muted, minimal or nonexistent. Conversely, if a terrorist attack in the Middle East occurs when gold is in a positive or bullish mode, then the gold market could surge higher. The time frame from 1999 through 2004 is one during which there is likely to be a significant confluence of events.

Warning: Regardless of the specific event or events that affect metals prices, the fact remains that investments in the metals have always been, and will likely continue to be, speculative and, therefore, subject to wide price fluctuations over both the long run and the short run. While many investment advisors tout the value of investing in precious metals as a hedge against uncertainty, it must be said that investing in precious metals is in and of itself uncertain at times. The vehicle that is thought to be the hedge against destabilizing and/or unexpected events is often unstable itself, and you must be prepared for this possibility. The correlation between metals prices and instability in markets or politics is not one-to-one.

CAVEAT EMPTOR

Because metals have attracted such a wide and faithful following among investors and speculators, they have also attracted a plethora of con artists, swindlers and other undesirables. The emotional response of investors to crisis and their flight to the perceived quality of metals has often caused scam artists to take advantage of investors. These individuals and firms have hatched literally hundreds of schemes designed to relieve investors of their money. The Y2K situation provides a natural vehicle for scam artists. Be careful not to get caught up in one of these tricky schemes. They are designed to achieve only one purpose—to separate you from your money by playing on the Y2K hysteria. As the Year 2000 approaches there will be more investment schemes, tricks, scams and pressures. You must avoid the panic that will surely increase as the end of the millennium approaches, and the new one begins.

While some of these programs are clearly illegal and fraudulent, others are on the fringe of legality, and still others are legal but based upon high-pressure sales tactics. While there are several ethical firms that specialize in strategic-metals investments, there are numerous fly-by-night firms that prey on public ignorance, greed and gullibility. There are many things these firms fail to tell you about the lack of liquidity in strategic-metals investments. Before you plunge into this area of metals investing, make sure you know what you're getting into, how easy it will be to get out, where your investments will be stored and how reliable your dealer is. As an investor or potential investor, you must always be cautious. "Investigate before you invest" always makes sense. It's a simple rule to follow, but when dealing in metals it's essential!

FUTURES AND OPTIONS

The risk of loss in futures and options trading is substantial. In fact, the odds of coming out ahead when buying futures options are slim to none. I am certain that as Y2K approaches you will see numerous programs touting options strategies. My advice is to investigate carefully before you invest a penny in such programs. Futures trading (as opposed to futures options) is preferable, but still risky and *not* suited to certain investors. Futures contracts are highly leveraged. The speculator is frequently required to use a margin of less than 5 percent of the total value of the underlying contract being traded. Leverage is a two-edged sword. It can work for you or it can work against you, but most often it tends to work against you.

Trading in futures options is more speculative than futures trading itself, since options have a limited lifespan. In fact, most futures options are totally worthless when they expire. Those who buy or sell options, as opposed to those who employ options strategies, rarely make money on their speculation. It is especially important, therefore, that you not place your money with a firm that specializes in metals-options trading only. The odds of success are minimal, and in most cases these firms charge large commissions (frequently several times larger than regular "full service" commissions). It often takes a very large move in the underlying metals futures contract just to make enough profit to pay your commissions.

OTHER METALS INVESTMENTS

Bullish markets in precious metals stimulate the growth of all sorts of metals investments. Among these are such things as gold-backed bonds and insurance. As with any investment, you must take the time and effort to investigate them thoroughly and carefully. I urge you to consult your accountant, attorney or investment advisor. Don't be afraid to ask specific questions, and don't hesitate to contact the proper government regulatory agencies to check on registrations, claims and credentials of firms and/or individuals with whom you are doing business.

No matter what the specific vehicle(s) may be, there is always risk. There is no such thing as a risk-free investment in precious metals. Don't let the fear of a millennium crash crisis fool you into an investment that's not suitable for you, no matter what the claims of its promoters may be.

Emotion has always been one of the primary driving forces in the metals markets, and it is emotion that prompts investors to become greedy or fearful. When greedy, the investor will take imprudent risks, making investments that are neither logical nor sound. Greed will drive an investor or speculator to remain with an investment too long, and greed will diminish judgment. Clearly, the possibility of a millennium crash is a major *potential* crisis. It has already aroused considerable emotion and will likely stimulate various types of hysteria.

Fear of losing money will cause investors to liquidate sound investments and to shy away from profitable opportunities. Whether you are involved in mining stocks, futures, options or other metals-related investments, you are more susceptible to the effects of fear than you would be in most other investments. Be aware of this and you will fare well. Forget my warnings or ignore them, and your odds of success will greatly diminish!

METALS MANIA

My first investment in stocks was made in 1968 while I was in my last year of college. With borrowed money I bought several hundred shares of Wright Hargreaves Mines (symbol WRT), a small Canadian gold producer. If memory serves me, the stock was in the $3 range. I recall with great fondness my excitement and anticipation. This, I felt, was the stock that would start me on my way to millions. I remember my trips to the local brokerage offices of what was then Hayden–Stone in Champaign, Illinois, and the tremendous anticipation I felt as I watched WRT move back and forth between $3 and $4 as it traded in sixteenths of a point.

A few years later the precious metals began major bull moves that culminated in all-time highs in 1980. The years between the late 1960s and the early 1980s marked one of the most volatile periods in the history of all metals prices. They also marked one of the most inflationary periods in U.S. history. Legalization of gold ownership by U.S. citizens during this period provided an additional buying impetus to hopeful investors.

Vast fortunes were made and lost during this two-decade span that was also, not surprisingly, characterized by unprecedented economic volatility and instability in virtually every corner of the world. Investors rushed into just about any proposition that involved metals. This was the age of the "gold bugs." Almost every investor, regardless of financial status, was interested in capitalizing on the fantastic opportunities still to be reaped. The average investor faced a choice of literally hundreds of different vehicles. The choices were further complicated by questions of timing, disagreement among the experts, unethical operators and extremely volatile international and domestic political and economic environments.

BEWARE OF "EXPERTS"

During this period literally hundreds of metals "experts" were born and grew to maturity seemingly overnight. While some, such as the late Verne Myers of Canada, the outspoken Harry Schultz and Jim Dines, were *bona fide* experts who were in on the "movement" well before its inception, many others sought to claim their fame riding on the coattails of the true experts. As the bull markets in precious metals pushed prices ever higher in what seemed to be a never-ending story, price projections and expectations increased as well. When the market peaks came in the early 1980s the buying frenzy was so intense that investors failed to see that the end was near. They were inspired by a plethora of bullish reports. Some experts claimed that gold prices would rise well in excess of $1000 an ounce and that silver would rally to $100 an ounce, as the Hunt brothers steadily increased their corner on the silver market. More recently we have heard of attempts by Warren Buffett to corner the silver market. As you know, the tops of the early 1980s developed when most investors were exceptionally optimistic. The tops coincided closely with buying panics. The developing Y2K crisis, or its aftermath, could serve as a powerful stimulus for a new and possibly historic metals mania.

During the days of metals mania, the investor was never quite sure where to turn. Would mining stocks be the best way to participate? After all, they paid dividends, and some of them had vast yet-untapped gold reserves. And if gold-mining stocks were the best vehicles, then which mines would be best? Would the Canadian mines do well, or was their cost of producing gold too high? Would South African mines be ideal since their cost of production was so much lower, or would they be too speculative due to the continuing racial unrest? And what about metals mutual funds? Which might perform best in the months and years ahead? Or would bullion coins be the way to go? Perhaps numismatic (rare) coins would be even better, since they combine the benefits of rarity with the attraction of precious metals.

As you can see, there are many questions about the correct way to invest in precious metals. Virtually every precious metals expert will have his or her recommended portfolio and strategy for Y2K and beyond. While some will push mutual funds, coins and gold-backed bonds, others will favor a healthy selection of penny-mining stocks. As always, the experts will disagree with one another, and this will prove confusing to the public. One thing that a majority of experts will agree on is the fact that precious metals are headed higher and higher. And the closer prices come to their tops, the more bullish the experts become. Those of us who have planned ahead will have gotten in at relatively low prices and will be exiting at the peak of the hysteria when the markets are topping.

LESSONS FROM METALS MANIAS PAST

When and if the precious metals buying spree comes, it will be important to remember that it has all happened before. And the lessons of history will be important. There have been numerous periods throughout economic history during which precious metals have been considered the premier investment panacea. Similar emotions and mass hysteria characterized each of these periods. The history of metals has been cyclical. While the cycles have not been predictable to the very day or month, all of the more widely known metals, such as copper, silver and gold, have had lengthy cyclical histories.

Various researchers, including E. R. Dewey, the Foundation for the Study of Cycles and others, have demonstrated the cyclical phenomenon in metals prices. My own research has confirmed the existence of these cycles, not only in the metals themselves, but in metal-shares prices as well. In-depth studies suggest that the cyclical patterns in metals may be nothing more than a reflection of underlying economic cycles, but even if this is the case, the validity of cycles in metals prices is not undermined.

Knowledge of the various cyclical patterns in metals is important. It can alert you to the approximate high and low turning points in these markets. Timing is critical in virtually all investments, but there are several other ingredients essential to success. Knowing that something will happen is important, but knowing what to do about it may be even more important.

Knowing when metals are likely to turn higher or lower is potentially quite valuable; however, it must be translated into a plan of action that will maximize dollar return on the information. What's more, knowledge of the market cycles and patterns will help temper your emotional response to metals. In a rising market, not all investment vehicles move at the same pace. In a falling market, not all investment vehicles drop so quickly or so far; some may even rise. Knowledge of these patterns will help you respond if and when the Y2K crisis develops.

LESSONS FROM THE CONTRARIANS

Market history is a reflection of human history. Human behavior, human attitudes and human emotion are key elements at major turning points in economic, social, political and speculative trends. When human sentiment is strongly aligned in one direction, there is a significant likelihood that the majority will be wrong. If you examine the role of sentiment during the Dutch Tulip Mania or before and during the crashes of 1929 and 1987, you will find that sentiment was strongly positive, that the public was clearly optimistic, bullish, positive and euphoric about the future. If you examine public and professional sentiment at major economic lows and market bottoms, or near changes in downtrends, you will find a pervasive negativism, a plurality of bears and a majority of sellers. This is common. This is how sentiment alerts astute traders and investors to changes in trends.

Students of the stock market have studied "odd lot" behavior for many years. When most small nonprofessional speculators are bearish and sell short, uneven lots of stock (under 100 shares), there is reason to believe that stocks are bottoming. R. E. Hadady developed what he called "The Bullish Consensus," a means of determining professional market consensus every week in order to gauge the level of bullish or bearish sentiment. In his book *Contrary Opinion,* Hadady made the following assumptions about strong levels of consensus among the professional market watchers whose collective opinions he tracked weekly:

> Contrary Opinion, perhaps the most powerful of all tools for predicting the future course of events in business and economics, is more often than not misunderstood and incorrectly applied. Contrary Opinion is, in essence, an opinion that it is contrary to what almost all of the people believe the course of events will be. In a given market, if almost all of the people believe that the prices will rise, the contrarian will be expecting prices to go down . . . equally applicable in all areas of business and economics . . . when the consensus of speculators reaches one of the two extremes, i.e., when almost everyone is bullish (expects prices to rise) or bearish (expects prices to decline).*

In 1987 I initiated a sentiment indicator that monitors the daily market sentiment of the trading public rather than relying on the weekly assessment of newsletters and brokerage houses. Instead of assessing the opinions of market professionals on a weekly basis as Hadady did, I weight my daily survey to the individual trader, deriving my data from a variety of individuals and sources. I have found that strongly positive sentiment tends to correlate highly with market peaks while strongly negative sentiment tends to correlate strongly with market lows.

How does this relate to coming Y2K crisis? The answer should be fairly obvious. When, prior to the Y2K crisis, most investors are excit-

---

* Hadady, R. E., *Contrary Opinion.* Pasadena, CA: Hadady Corp., 1983, p. 1.

ed, euphoric and bullish, trends are likely to be topping. When most people are most negative about Y2K, when panic reigns supreme, the worst will be close to an end.

When sentiment runs high (more than 90 percent agreement), you are most likely to profit by taking action in the opposite direction. The greater the public's positive sentiment, the more likely we are to be near an economic peak; the greater the public's negativism, the more likely we are to be near an economic low. It's that simple. Though not infallible, the degree of sentiment is an important indicator, one I suggest you follow closely. Mass hysteria is likely if and when Y2K problems develop. When this hysteria reaches a severe level and forecasts are the most negative is when the crisis will end.

What You Need to Know to Invest in Precious Metals

Most average investors are unfamiliar with the metals markets. To understand the many obstacles you face when investing in the metals markets as one part of your millennium strategy, you will need to:

1. *Understand the general aspects of each market.* There are important facts about the metals that are not generally known. A working knowledge of the basics of each major metals market will assist you in planning your protective portfolio.

2. *Learn if, how and when to invest in each market.* While some metals are ideal investment vehicles, others are not, since they are not in short supply or heavy demand. Still other metals prices are tightly controlled by a small group of producers or suppliers. These metals may or may not be suitable for investors; some may never be liquid enough to be suitable for any investor at any time. What's more, you will need to know not only which metals to buy but how to buy them and how they react during periods of extreme volatility and emotion.

3. *Know the various investment vehicles available to you,* including stocks, futures, options, coins, mutual funds and others. While you may know a little about each of these vehicles, you will want to know which of these choices is best for you, and when. Clearly, you will want to have some degree of diversification when the economic crisis develops. This information will help you develop a balanced portfolio of holdings.

4. *Plan a strategy for future moves in the metals markets.* While I will answer many of your questions, since individual circumstances differ, I cannot possibly answer all of them. However, there are numerous sources to which you can turn for assistance. I also recommend that you consult with your investment advisor, financial planner, broker or tax consultant.

However, remember that opinions about the direction or expected direction of the metals markets are only opinions. While it may be reasonable to solicit their input regarding how much money you should commit, how much risk you can take or what the tax consequences of your investments might be, you might want to ignore their input about the anticipated direction of the markets since their knowledge and studies may not be so intense or so complete as yours.

Summary

Remember that investing in metals is highly emotional. The psychology of investing is a field unto itself. While you may have done a thorough job of researching and preparing your plan, you may fail if you lack the discipline to implement it thoroughly, consistently and without the fear and greed that often prove to be the undoing of otherwise successful programs. Keep your emotions in check and be aware of your motivation for taking specific actions at given times.

In this chapter, I have attempted to provide as much information as possible about each of the metals; however, conditions change rapidly in our modern world. Technology is growing at an exponential pace and with it new applications for metals are found virtually every day. Recently, for example, researchers have introduced a powerful new drug for cancer treatment that uses platinum as its base. While the use of certain metals is declining, applications for other metals are on the rise. Although some of the specifics may change, the fundamentals of investing in metals will likely never be out of date. As long as human beings continue to advance their technology, metals will continue to play an essential role in their efforts.

We have seen wars come and go in recent years. We have seen petroleum crises, economic crises, terrorist attacks, stock market panics, the economic collapse of Russia, the investigation of President

Clinton and more. None of these has resulted in more than a minor up move in gold. The market has told us that it is waiting for a much more severe development in order for it to move higher. The Y2K crisis seems to be a perfect fit. Only time will tell. However, as long as you keep in mind the fact that metals are responsive to extremes in emotion, and extremes in emotion are a function of market conditions, you will do well. When emotions and markets appear to be out of control, and traders and investors are in a frenzy, precious metals become the preferred investments. Emotional markets are difficult to control or predict; however, they have established certain correlates over the years. One of these is the fact that metals will move as a result of emotional extremes. Once we understand this, we can use it to our advantage.

INVESTING IN METALS STOCKS AND FUTURES

There are many different vehicles for investing in the metals. Since the day-to-day prices of precious metals are more commonly followed, there are numerous investment opportunities in gold, silver, platinum and palladium.

A self-contained nation is a backward nation, with large numbers of people either permanently out of work, or very poorly paid in purchasing power. A nation which trades freely with all the world, selling to others those commodities which it can best produce, and buying from others those commodities which others can best produce, is by far the best conditioned nation . . .

—Walter Parker

What follows is a working overview of what is available, as well as some of the pros and cons of each approach. For more information, contact either a reputable broker and/or up-to-date reference sources. The world of investment alternatives is not static. Every day brings new and exciting opportunities; however, opportunity also brings risk, and the risks are not just financial.

There are always unscrupulous promoters, dishonest brokers and illegal schemes, all of which are designed to separate investors from their funds. Fortunately, they are in the minority, but you should still thoroughly investigate the credentials of every promoter, broker or manager of any program or plan you intend to follow. Some of the potential pitfalls will be pointed out to you as we discuss the various ways to invest in this market.

Investing in Metals Shares

The single most popular way to invest in metals is through the shares market, but there are so many different mining companies, so many choices facing the investor, that knowing which to buy, when and why is complex. While it is often assumed that rising metals prices will be reflected in the rising price of mining company shares, this is not always the case. Nor is it true that falling metals prices will be reflected in the declining price of shares.

The production costs, ore reserves, debt structure and operating expenses of every producer are distinctly different. The cost of mining gold in Canada, for example, is substantially different from that in South Africa. And the location of ore reserves for each producer varies significantly, making it more (or less) costly for some producers to extract their metals.

There are also such considerations as long-term reserves, the grade of ore being mined, the experience of corporate management and competitive producers. Only study and analysis can ascertain the importance of such factors. This is where patience, research and knowledge of financial analysis can be very helpful. On the other hand, you could ignore the fundamentals and analyze stocks strictly on a technical basis, using charts and price and/or trading-volume data.

If you are not prepared to do all the research yourself, there are numerous investment advisory services that provide specific recommendations on mining shares. In selecting a service to help you analyze mining stocks, you should consider both the amount of funds you have available and the nature of the service. Is it a conservative or an aggressive service? Is it a service geared to penny-mining shares, other highly speculative stocks or some of the better-known stocks?

Consider also whether you want to invest in American, Canadian, South African or Australian shares, or a combination of these. Although it is true that some of the more speculative stocks can appreciate dramatically in a bull market, it is also true that these shares often decline in price and your money will be lost. A mix of shares is often best;

however, I suggest you concentrate primarily on the more established producers, particularly those listed on the New York Stock Exchange, the American Stock Exchange, some OTC issues and some of the Toronto Stock Exchange Shares. For more speculative issues, consider the South African mines, but again, try to stay with those that have well-established operations.

For those who do not wish to do the analysis and study necessary to select mining shares, I recommend some of the mutual funds. Although there are fees involved, the portfolios of these funds are highly diversified and your return could be very good with little or no effort on your part in terms of selecting the individual stocks to buy or sell. The only thing you'll need to concern yourself with is timing.

DOLLAR-COST AVERAGING METHOD

One of the most sensible approaches to dealing with the issue of timing purchases and sales is to use a dollar-cost averaging technique. While this approach is not recommended for futures or other margin-type accounts, it can be very effective when purchasing stocks. Dollar-cost averaging is the technique we use to compensate for the fact that our timing in buying metals stocks may be too early, too late or otherwise incorrect. None of us can know exactly when bull markets will begin or when bear markets will end. Although such methods as technical and/or fundamental analysis can help, they're far from perfect.

Dollar-cost averaging is really a simple technique that can be applied to many different types of investments. There are several methods of cost averaging. The simplest is to invest a predetermined amount in stocks, coins, etc., on a regular schedule. The interval could be monthly, bimonthly, semiannually or otherwise. In a falling market, each purchase brings the average cost of your investment closer to the mean, or average, price, which will decline steadily in a falling market. Hence, you will be slowly but surely lowering your average price. When prices begin to turn higher, your average cost will be low compared to current prices, and you will have accumulated a large investment (relative to your finances and needs) at what is, one hopes, a reasonably low price.

As you can see, a lot of the decision making is avoided by the use of such a regular purchasing program. Naturally, when the market begins its upswing, you would cease your buying in order not to raise your cost too high and thereby defeat the purpose of your cost-averaging program. However, you may not be able to tell that the market has started its major upswing and, as a result, you may not know whether to stop your program of accumulation.

PURCHASE PROGRAM

This problem can be resolved by using a modified program, one that I prefer. Rather than purchase blindly every month, you could buy selectively based on price level. Say, for example, that you are interested in accumulating a position in silver-mining shares, but only when the price of the stock is low in comparison to its historical movements. You examine the price of the stock and observe that, since the 1950s, it has made several important bottoms in the $8 to $11 price range. Currently the price is at $14 per share, and silver prices are falling, along with the price of most mining shares.

Your program might, therefore, be to buy 20 shares every month (although I'd recommend at least 100-share blocks in order to save on commission charges) as long as the price of the stock is at $11 or lower. Or you might give yourself a little leeway and buy only if the price is at $12 or lower. If the price is not in your target range one month, you might save the funds and double or triple your purchase the next time the price enters your predetermined range. This type of selective dollar-cost averaging is, I feel, a sensible long-term approach to investing in metals shares. (It can also be used with metals mutual funds.)

You might decide to cost-average on the sell side as well. In other words, you might establish your target range for liquidating shares or mutual funds. This is not necessarily a bad approach; however, you must remember that declining markets fall much more quickly than rising markets rise. In other words, a bull market of several years' duration can be erased in a matter of several weeks, or even less. Your liquidation program will, in view of this well-established fact of life, need to be much more aggressive and shorter term. You might modify your program to take advantage of positive news in a given stock or in the general market, liquidating fairly large portions of your holdings on price strength.

DIVIDENDS OR CAPITAL GAINS

There are at least two schools of thought about metals investments. On the one hand, there are those who will tell you that you ought to consider dividends in deciding which stocks to buy, sell or hold. I say that if you want dividends, you ought to put your money into vehicles that will give you dividends. I regard metals investments as primarily speculative. While there are reasonable dividends to be had from the larger, more-established gold and copper producers, and from some of the more conservative mutual funds, investing in precious metals is primarily a game of capital appreciation.

Your decision as to which shares to buy, or which metals vehicles to invest in, should be based on the idea that capital appreciation is your primary goal. Although the stability and other fundamentals of the investments you ultimately choose are important considerations, your decision should not take dividends into account. The overwhelming percentage of your profits or losses will occur as a function of price swings and not as a result of dividends.

Futures Trading in Metals

While it is true that futures trading is one of the most speculative ways to participate in the markets, it is also one of the most potentially rewarding. Furthermore, futures trading requires a relatively small investment, inasmuch as margin requirements are in the area of 1 to 5 percent compared with the almost 50 percent margin requirement in stocks. (I suggest you read this chapter thoroughly before you attempt to speculate in metals futures. Those who are already familiar with futures trading may wish to go on to the next chapter.)

HOW FUTURES TRADING WORKS

The futures market is, in many respects, similar to the stock market. There are, however, a number of significant differences. While the stock investor or speculator who purchases shares has a virtually unlimited amount of time to hold those shares, the futures trader does not. This is because futures transactions involve specific delivery times, after which the contract buyer must purchase the actual tangible commodity unless the contract has been sold to another trader.

(We've all heard of the mythical futures trader who forgot that he had bought live cattle futures and awoke one morning to find that 40,000 pounds of live beef steers had been delivered to his home. Naturally, this is pure fiction. In reality this does not occur. While speculators are "called for delivery," the actual commodity is not delivered until the balance of it has been paid for, and when it is delivered, it is sent to a predetermined location such as a feed lot, storage vault or grain elevator, depending on the commodity.)

HOW THE PROCESS WORKS

Assume that you believe gold prices are going to increase. Assume also that your capital is limited to $5000. You would have several choices regarding the allocation of your resources. You could buy 200 shares of a moderately priced gold stock and spend perhaps $2400. Assuming a 50 percent margin, you might only spend $1200. You might decide to take more risk and buy several thousand shares of a "penny-mining stock." It's a long shot, but if you are right in your stock selection, you could increase your funds by as much as several thousand percent.

Of course, you would also know that the probability of such profits actually being made in penny-mining shares is rather low. I am not suggesting here that you cannot be successful in penny-mining shares. I am merely reaffirming the fact that the odds of profitable penny-stock investing are low and that the mines could easily go out of business. You could decide to place some funds in coins; however, you cannot do so on margin and you would, therefore, not have any leverage.

Assume, however, that you are interested in buying gold futures in order to maximize your available capital. Before doing this you should make sure that all funds used for futures trading are strictly *risk capital* and that your lifestyle will not be adversely affected if it were all lost. You also need to know that in futures trading you could lose more than you invest. This is so because at 1 to 5 percent margin you are controlling a large amount of a commodity with a small amount of capital. Should the market move against you (that is, down if you have bought, or up if you have sold short), then you might lose more than what you have invested.

DECIDING TO INVEST IN FUTURES

Now that you understand the risks, you decide to go ahead with your trading. Since you have concluded that gold prices are likely to rise, you decide to buy gold futures. Although gold futures are traded at a number of futures exchanges throughout the world, the primary market is in New York at the COMEX exchange. The gold-futures contract at the COMEX has particular specifications, as do all futures contracts. It calls for the delivery of 100 troy ounces of gold, and there are specific delivery months in gold, just as there are in all futures contracts. A delivery month specifies an exact date at which the contract buyer will pay the contract seller the balance of the funds due.

If, for example, you buy gold futures at $300 per ounce, the total contract value would be $300 times 100 ounces, or $30,000. The margin on this transaction would be approximately $1500 (this amount will vary from one brokerage firm to another). As prices rise, your firm might require more margin money, since the contract value would increase. Remember that the $1500 margin is not your only risk. You could lose more. Here's how. At 100 ounces per contract, a one-dollar decline in gold prices equals a $100 decline in the contract value.

A $15 drop in gold prices below your purchase price would equal a $1500 decline in your funds. Your margin money would be gone if you sold your contract at $15 lower than your purchase price. However, if the market declined $25 from your entry price, which could happen quickly, you would not only lose your $1500, but you'd owe the broker an additional $1000. If you did not send the additional funds, usually within 48 hours, your broker would sell your position at whatever price could be had, and you'd still owe the additional money.

Remember, however, that things could also work the other way. A $25 rise in gold prices from your purchase price translates into a $2500 paper profit for you. A $30 rise in gold prices from your entry price would mean that you had doubled your original capital, provided, of course, that you sold your contract.

Additional details.   There are various "delivery months" in all futures markets. In COMEX gold futures, the delivery months are February, April, June, August, October and December. The contract specifications for each futures market define the exact delivery date, delivery location and details of the product to be delivered (such as grade, purity, etc.). At the end of the month prior to the delivery month, speculators who do not intend to complete the transaction by actually accepting delivery of the underlying commodity must close out their positions. If they do not, their broker will receive a "delivery notice" and will then inform the customer. The contract must then be sold immediately or delivery will be made and the additional amount due will be debited to the customer's account.

Since a completed futures transaction costs the speculator a commission, it is in the best interest of the speculator to buy the contract month that will conform most closely to the anticipated length of the market move. Because commissions are relatively low in futures, however, it is best to trade during the nearby delivery months, as opposed to the distant, or "deferred," months. This is because trading activity is larger in the nearby months and, as a consequence, it is easier to buy or sell because of the substantially larger volume of trading (called liquidity).

As you can see, the leverage in futures trading is exceptionally large. This leverage can be used to your advantage, but it can also work against you. By using leverage effectively, by cutting losses, by fine-tuning your timing to pinpoint accuracy and by riding profits, you can be extremely successful in futures trading. Yet the risks are substantial. A well-planned investment program should include a portion of funds dedicated to futures trading, but I urge all metals investors to diversify their funds among a variety of investment vehicles.

Futures Markets in Metals

GOLD FUTURES

As noted earlier, gold futures are traded at the COMEX exchange in New York. The COMEX contract calls for a minimum of 100 troy ounces of gold. A 50-troy-ounce contract is traded in Chicago at the Mid-America Commodity Exchange, and gold futures are traded at numerous other exchanges the world over. Delivery months for COMEX gold have been noted above. The COMEX contract is the major gold futures market and is the one that should be traded, unless your funds are limited and the 50-ounce contract is more suited to your pocketbook.

SILVER FUTURES

These, too, are traded in New York at the COMEX exchange. The contract size is 5000 ounces. This translates to $50 per one-cent move in silver prices. In other words, if you buy COMEX silver futures at $4.75 per ounce, and the price increases to $4.76 per ounce, then you have a $50 paper profit. A $1 increase in silver prices amounts to a $5000 profit. While there is also a 1000-ounce contract traded in Chicago at the Chicago Board of Trade, the most active silver-futures market is at the COMEX. Silver futures are also traded throughout the world at various exchanges.

PLATINUM FUTURES

Platinum futures are traded in New York at the NYMEX. The contract calls for delivery of 50-troy-ounces of platinum. A $1 move in the price of platinum, therefore, is equivalent to a $50 move in the futures contract. Delivery months for platinum futures are January, April, July and October. Although platinum futures are also traded in London, trading volume at all exchanges is considerably less in platinum than in either silver or gold.

Because of the relatively low trading activity in platinum futures and the volatile nature of this market, I advise considerable caution, unless you are an experienced futures trader. While this may change as interest in platinum increases, you should be aware that this market has a history of considerable volatility characterized by wide price swings.

PALLADIUM FUTURES

Like platinum, palladium futures are traded in New York at the MYMEX. The contract calls for delivery of 100-troy-ounces of palladium. A $1 move in palladium prices is equivalent, therefore, to a $100 move in the futures contract. Palladium is the most thinly traded of the precious metals. In fact, the market is so thin (i.e., inactive) that I do not advise novice traders to speculate in palladium futures. If you do, make certain that you understand the types of orders to give your broker to ensure the best price executions.

As investors the world over begin to recognize the importance and explosive price potential of palladium, due both to its supply characteristics and growing demand, the futures market is likely to become considerably more active.

Analyzing the Metals Markets

The futures speculator has a number of alternatives when it comes to making decisions about the markets. There are, as in stocks, two distinct approaches to market selection and timing. The fundamental approach, in its purest sense, involves studying the basics of supply and demand. The statistics used by fundamental analysts include such factors as production data, consumption data, warehouse stocks, consumer demand, industrial consumption, exports, imports, mining statistics and a host of other significant variables. In addition, the fundamentalist must also consider such things as international and domestic political events, relationships to other markets and even such things as natural catastrophes and weather.

The purely technical trader, on the other hand, has little or no interest in the fundamental data. Market technicians study price trends, trading activity, futures-contract open interest and a host of mathematical manipulations of this data. Technicians also study price-chart patterns according to principles and techniques discussed in the classic text on chart analysis by Edwards and McGee.*

While there are many strictly fundamental traders and possibly even more technical traders, most futures traders apply a hybrid approach to their trade selection. They are not entirely committed to one extreme or another. Rather, they use their knowledge of technical patterns to improve market timing when the fundamentals suggest that a significant price move is likely to develop.

Still other traders will not align themselves with either camp. Instead, they'll subscribe to one or more of the many newsletters and advisory services, and follow those recommendations instead of doing their own research.

---

* Edwards, Robert D. and John Magee, *Technical Analysis of Stock Trends.* Boston, MA: John Magee Inc., 1981.

There is nothing wrong with this approach as long as you take note of the following caveats:

1. *Research the performance history* of the newsletter or trading advisor whose recommendations you plan to follow.

2. *Look for consistency of performance,* rather than exceptionally high percentage returns alternating with large down swings in performance. You are much better off taking the recommendations of a service or advisor who has had average, but consistent, performance than one who has had large up and down swings. Consistency of performance will help ensure that you are not entering the program prior to one of the large drawdowns in performance.

3. *Take the advice of a service that specializes in precious metals* as opposed to one that gives recommendations on all futures markets.

4. *Don't listen to too many advisors.* While it is natural to seek as much input and advice as you can possibly get, there are some pitfalls to listening to too many advisors. The most obvious pitfall is confusion. My best advice is to find several advisors whose work you are pleased with and then follow their advice, or formulate your own plan based on your analysis of their advice.

5. *Use just one advisory service, but don't pick and choose from among the recommendations of that service.* Many investors find that they pick the recommendations that don't work more often than they pick the ones that do work. Exactly why this is so I'm not sure; however, it seems to be a fact of market life.

6. *Start with a service when it has had a losing streak.* All too often investors are attracted to a trading advisor or an advisory service when the results of the service have been exceptionally good. Frequently this is the same time that the service begins to give back some of its profits. Therefore, you are far better off tracking a service for an extended period of time and following its recommendations when its results have been on the down swing for a while.

7. *Decide on your approach to the markets.* Will it be long term, short term or intermediate term? Try not to switch time frames; instead, segregate your trades into categories and then follow them up accordingly.

DO IT YOURSELF OR HIRE A MONEY MANAGER?

While many investors hope to achieve success in metals futures independently, this is not realistic. Success in futures, metals or otherwise, is difficult to achieve. A vast majority of futures traders lose their risk capital, and they tend to lose it rather quickly. The few who do achieve success are often very successful, and therein lies the attraction for those who decide to invest in futures.

In the long run, you may be better off selecting a money manager or trading advisor to handle your precious metals futures trading for you. While there are not many money managers who trade only in precious metals, there are some who do. You can find them by doing a little research.

There are two alternatives:

1. Place your investment with a professionally managed futures fund. The publicly-offered funds and/or limited partnerships are reviewed regularly either in *Futures Magazine* or *Managed Account Reports*. If you take this approach, do your homework and find a program with the following characteristics:

- *Longevity*—Look for a fund that has been in operation for at least 10 years.

- *Steady growth*—Over time, this approach is preferable to large up and down swings.

- *No more than 50 percent drawdown*—"Maximum drawdown" is the amount of dollar decline from a high point. A fund may show net asset value of $5000 per unit and then drop to $2000 per unit, before moving to $10,000. In the interim the investor may lose faith and drop out of the program. Large drawdowns are difficult for most investors to accept, and they tend to drop out of programs when the drawdown becomes large, although this is often at the bottom of the decline.

  Large drawdowns are also dangerous, since most funds have a provision that requires them to stop trading once a certain percentage of funds has been lost. The more frequent the large drawdown, the greater the danger that the program will not recover.

- *Reasonable management fees*—Some funds have built in a host of management fees, profit incentives and commission charges that are bottom-line losses to the investor. Carefully study the charges of each fund or program and compare them with other programs. Make certain that the commission charges are reasonable, or look for discount commissions. Commission charges can add up to a major burden on fund performance.

2. Place funds with an individual account manager.   The caveats are the same as those given above. *Managed Account Reports* (MAR) can help you evaluate some of these programs; however, many of them are not examined by MAR. In such cases, you must carefully examine the disclosure document of each program. This is a document required by the Commodity Futures Trading Commission and the National Futures Association.

Before you place a single penny with an account manager, study the disclosure document carefully and ask questions about anything you don't understand. The same general guidelines as those given above for futures funds are applicable to individually managed accounts.

OTHER CONSIDERATIONS IN FUTURES TRADING

There are numerous other precautions a successful trader must take:

1. Real-time performance record essential.   If you plan to trade for yourself using a technical trading approach, find or develop a trading system that has a real-time performance record (or computer-tested record if real time is not available) of at least 60 percent profitable trades, with a ratio of approximately 2 to 1 in terms of dollars made versus dollars lost per trade (including commissions as losses). These criteria could also apply to individually managed futures accounts or futures funds.

In the absence of real-time results, computer results are acceptable if you have made provisions for the limitations (i.e., drawdown). (Although these figures need not be adhered to exactly, they should be used as minimum guidelines in evaluating both the performance of a technical trading system as well as the performance of a managed account or futures fund.)

2. Understand your time limitations.   The system you find or develop should be one that fits the limits of your available time (with or without a computer system). If the trading signals you plan to use are provided by an advisory service, then familiarize yourself with the trading system, its general principles, performance statistics, historical results and other details described previously in this chapter.

3. Choose a brokerage firm compatible with your needs.   If you are an independent trader who requires no trading advice whatsoever, then select a discount firm that gives prompt order executions. If, however, you are a novice trader, you may prefer to do business with a full-service firm where you will pay higher commissions in order to get the assistance you need.

4. Choose your broker carefully.   When choosing a particular broker within the brokerage firm, both you and the broker should be aware of each other's needs. The broker cannot serve you well unless he or she knows what you will require in the way of advice, price quotations, assistance with order placement, procedures, etc. Keep the lines of communication open.

5. Determine the amount of risk.   Make certain you have sufficient risk capital to trade the system you have selected. Your risk capital should be truly risk capital and not funds that you have borrowed or that have been allocated to a different program or need. I cannot overemphasize the importance of this point!

6. Formulate a coherent trading philosophy.   As you know, your perceptions of trading, your expectations, your goals and your market orientation (i.e., long-term, short-term, etc.) are all factors that contribute either to success or to failure.

Futures trading in the metals markets is often affected by strong emotions and volatile economic events. If you consider these events within the framework of a consistent and logical trading philosophy, you can integrate and understand these events and emotions more productively and more profitably.

7. Plan your trades and carry out your plans consistently. Avoid the temptation to make emotional decisions not based on your particular system or method.

8. Do your work in isolation.   When it comes to speculation, working alone forces you to make decisions based almost exclusively on your opinions and helps you avoid being distracted from your plan. You don't necessarily want anyone else's input or opinions. With experience and the confidence it brings, you will soon realize that your own opinions are just as valuable as the opinions of any other trader or market analyst. Some of the most successful traders work alone.

9. Treat futures trading as a serious business.   Before you begin, formulate rules, organizational procedures, goals and expectations. Delineate these carefully, within the limits of your abilities and expectations, both financial and personal.

10. Don't procrastinate.   Once your trading decisions have been made (whether the decision is to get into or out of a trade, whether you are taking a profit or exiting at a loss), act as soon as your system dictates action; no sooner, no later.

11. Limit your risk exposure and preserve capital.   The best way to limit risk is to trade in only three to six markets at a time and to avoid trading in markets that have swings too large for your account size. Since there are only four to five major futures markets in the metals, you will not need to worry about trading in too many futures markets.

Remember also that the precious metals tend to move together. Once you have decided to limit risk to a certain dollar amount or to limit risk using specific techniques, make sure you take your losses as soon as they reach that point. Riding losses is the most common, and the most costly, error made by futures traders.

12. Avoid anticipation.   Far too many traders go astray when they try to anticipate signals from their trading system. You cannot tell the market what to do. It will always move in the direction of least resistance, and your task is to follow the market through its endless twists and turns. If prices are trending higher, you should trade from the long side. If prices are trending lower, trade from the short side.

13. Evaluate your progress and results regularly.   Feedback is important to the futures trader. While the feedback will be obvious when you tally your profits and losses, the reasons for your profits or losses may not be clear if you wait too long to evaluate them. Study your results and, particularly, the specific behaviors that led to those results, good or bad.

14. Do your market work.   Whether you are a novice or a seasoned veteran, with or without a computer, you must keep up-to-date in your market studies. Futures markets move quickly, and there is often little time to update your trading signals once a move has occurred.

If you have a computer, then you can program it to automatically update your signals or system every day at a set time. If you do not use a computer to track your system, then you must set aside a certain time for your market work. You must keep your market analyses current.

15. Control your emotions.   The chief enemy of the speculator is emotion; however, the greatest friend of the speculator is the emotion of others. In futures trading, emotions must be kept under control. The consequences of emotionally based decisions can be very costly to the speculator since they often (but not always) result in unwarranted actions.

16. Don't take tips and don't give tips.   Trading futures is a lonely task. "Sure things," insider information and rumor are not consistent with systematic trading. We are all tempted to find the easy way, but the easy way is rarely the best way. Avoid the temptation to take tips, to seek out inside information, to listen to the opinions of other traders or to believe that the people you are listening to know more than you do.

Sometimes they do, but most of the time they don't. Collective opinions are, of course, helpful in the case of contrary opinion studies, but individual opinions or tips are most often counterproductive to the trader.

17. Trade with your winnings.   When you have enjoyed a particularly successful period, it is a good idea to remove money from your account. Whether you do this on a profitable-trade basis or on a time basis (i.e., daily, weekly, monthly) is not important. What's important is to siphon money from your account so that you are in a position to trade with your winnings after having taken your start-up capital out of the markets. Futures traders have winning and losing streaks.

During the winning streaks, profits often accumulate rapidly. You may become so impressed with your own success that you try to expand your trading. While there will be a time to expand your trading and to increase the size of your position, it is usually not wise to do so when you are feeling euphoric about your performance. I recommend that you withdraw funds monthly. (Your broker might not take kindly to your removing profits following every profitable trade.)

18. Develop winning attitudes and behaviors. Study the lives and works of great traders. The essential variable in successful trading is the trader, not the system. A good trader can make virtually any system work.

19. "The trend is your friend." This wise old bit of market wisdom is known to many, but understood and used by few. Be cautious when your trades are not consistent with the existing trend. There will be times when your signals will be contrary to the trend; however, you must always be careful about trades and signals that go against the primary trend, since they will most often be wrong.

The rules I have given you are based on my experiences and observations in futures trading since 1968. While these rules are applicable to all traders, they may be more important to those involved in the metals markets than to other futures traders. The emotion, patience and tenacity required to trade in metals futures is considerable. Although some rules may be more important to some individuals than to others, I know that at one time or another, each of these rules will be important to all traders.

The most effective way to put these rules into action and to internalize them is to study them, keep them handy and review them frequently. They are intended to keep you on the right track, and they will help keep you honest with yourself. You must never forget that one of the most serious blunders a speculator can commit is self-deception. To refuse to accept a loss is to invite failure. It is impossible to trade futures without taking losses. No trader or speculator is immune to losses. Ultimately what separates the winners from the losers in futures trading and in most investment areas is the ability to be honest with oneself. From a clear perception of market reality grows the skill to recognize what is important and valuable in the markets and to discard what is useless and meaningless.

Suggested Precious Metals Portfolio

Many market analysts overestimated the role and value of precious metals in the 1970s. They erred in thinking that the up swing in precious metals would last forever. The cast of characters in the "Gold Follies of the 1970s" included some of the best-known names in the investment business. Some forecasts published in the 1970s were outrageously bullish. A sizable majority of analysts were most bullish at the top. Fortunately, the more sensible and well-established advisors retained their good sense and advised caution or liquidation when prices were rocketing skyward seemingly with no end in sight.

Yet a few actors in this tragic comedy were unabashedly bullish and remained bullish as the roller coaster plummeted earthward. These characters will go unnamed; they have suffered enough. Yet they seem to resurface with every brief upturn in precious metals, once again ready to peddle their undying bullish forecasts to the public. Their failure, in addition to poor judgment, was in closing their eyes and ears to the economic realities of precious metals as commodities that move up and down in response to inflation and disinflation.

A more rational point of view on the precious metals follows. Donald Hoppe, whose work I hold in the highest esteem, notes:

> But when gold is undervalued, as it was in the 1920s, before the devaluation of 1934, and again in the 1960s, before the abandonment of the fixed $35 per ounce gold parity for the dollar, gold mines were going out of business. There is little profit in mining gold when operating costs are high and the price of the metal (that is, its purchasing power) is low. On the other hand, in the late 1970s and thus far into the '80s, gold has not only increased in price, but has become overvalued (again in terms of its purchasing power). I agree it is not as overvalued as it was at its all-time high of $850 per ounce ...
>
> In any case, could it be that the price of gold has become inflated along with everything else? Remember, for the first time in the history of money, gold, since 1973, has been freely traded, and its price has been set by the market rather than by government fiat. And if the market has now overvalued gold, will the market not ultimately correct this error—or even make the contrary error of undervaluing it in the future?*

What follows are some observations on what may happen in the precious metals market that may help you establish a precious metals portfolio. Actual events may cause you to modify your actions.

1. *The profit potential of precious metals during a deflating or disinflating economy will be limited unless prices are fixed by*

---

* Hoppe, Donald, *Kondratieff Wave Analyst.* Crystal Lake, IL: 1988, p. 24.

government mandate or decree. If the U.S. government moves to increase gold reserves or otherwise acts to buy gold, bolstering U.S. dollar strength, then precious metals will increase in value regardless of the underlying economic trend, particularly if purchases are heavy. I do not consider this a particularly realistic possibility at the present time.

2. *If the U.S. government decides to print its way out of debt, then inflation will explode* and with it the price of all commodities, whether foods, metals, livestock or fibers. All markets are then likely to move higher, and precious metals will be favored.

3. *In the event of a serious banking crisis, precious metals may increase in value;* however, the need to own precious metals well in advance of such a crisis is mitigated by their probable disinflationary decline. Therefore, it may be best to buy precious metals at the inception of such a crisis, but not until then.

4. *In the event of a serious military confrontation, precious metals could increase in value.*

5. *During the disinflationary stage of the long wave, I recommend that no more than 20 percent of your portfolio be in precious metals.*

6. *Of that 20 percent, I recommend:* approximately 30 percent gold, 40 percent platinum, 20 percent palladium and the balance in silver.

7. *This distribution will change as the long wave begins its up swing and as the up swing approaches its later stages.*

Alternatives to Precious Metals

This book is not intended to serve as a step-by-step investment guide to the precious metals. There are, however, several suggestions I can give you, based on my personal experience and observations.

MINING STOCKS

These have long been a favorite of investors. Whether Canadian, U.S., South African or Australian mining shares, this aspect of the precious metals market has always fascinated speculators and investors. As you

know, there are investment-grade mining stocks and there are speculative mining stocks. There will always be the potential to make and/or
lose fortunes in speculative stocks, but I consider them too risky for
most investors.

Those who favor stocks over bullion point to the most incredible
rise in Homestake Mining during the Depression of the 1930s. This
was, of course, due to a special situation; namely, the price of gold was
fixed, and investors flocked into the shares market as an alternative,
since owning gold was not legal in the United States. Will this happen
again? If it does, then gold shares will be a worthwhile investment.*

BULLION

Bullion coins are probably the most sensible way for the investor to
participate. They are readily bought and sold, they need not be assayed
or verified as to content and they are well known throughout the
world. There are gold, silver, platinum and palladium bullion coins.
Remember to do business with a reputable and established dealer.

I do not recommend bullion in the form of bars or ingots for the
average investor. It takes time to sell bullion, it must be reassayed and
it is generally not so popular or so liquid a medium as bullion coins.

FUTURES AND OPTIONS

These vehicles are for the most speculative investors, those with large
amounts of risk capital. In the proper economic environment, inflating
or deflating, the disciplined trader can acquire a vast fortune speculating in futures; however, there is also the distinct possibility of loss. The
fact is that more than 90 percent of all futures speculators lose. The
odds are clearly against you. But if you have some risk capital, if the
time is right and if your timing is on target, you stand to make it big.

PRECIOUS METALS MUTUAL FUNDS

This may be the best way to go if you're interested in stocks but if you
haven't the time or the inclination to follow all of the stocks.

---

* It should be noted that there may be problems associated with the ownership of South
African gold shares.

There will be a time and a place for precious metals. Metals make up only part of your investment portfolio; however, during times of disinflation the role of metals will be one of minimal importance. It should be noted, as mentioned earlier, that precious metals are in their Stage 9 bottoming phase, or they may have already bottomed. A new bull market may be prompted by a Y2K crisis.

The precise economic stimulus for the expected up swing is uncertain; however, it could very well be the result of banking problems. If this is the case, then investors should prepare for up swing by taking a more aggressive stance when the cycles begin to turn higher. Refer to the gold, silver and platinum cycles charts for specifics. Above all, don't allow yourself to become a precious metals fanatic. Take a common sense viewpoint. Put only a portion of your assets into precious metals, and do so when the "buy" signals are there.

Summary

Finally, I urge all who wish to trade metals futures to remember the risks at all times. As you achieve success, as you see your positions proven correct, as you watch your profits grow, there will be an ever-increasing urge to pyramid your trading, to add more and more positions to the paper profits you have accumulated. This is not good practice. More often than not such practices will erase all of your profits as soon as the market turns against you. Your pyramid must be largest at the start of a move so that it will have a strong base of support.

PREPARE;
AVOID THE IMPACT

The coming MC will not be a pretty sight. The euphoria that marked the biggest bull market in history will first give way to panic and fear,

> It is impossible today to forecast the impact of this event, and the range of possibilities runs from minimal to extremely serious...*
>
> –Edward W. Kelley, Jr.

and then to persistent declines and lengthy periods of economic contraction. When the end comes it will lead to a chain reaction of events, all of which have been seen before, but few of which were expected. It is the supposedly "unexpected" nature of things that will act to instill fear and suffering in the lives of investors. Many will make serious mistakes. Some will be saved by quick and intelligent actions, but still more will be seriously and irreparably hurt. But who will be hurt the most? It's not necessary to be a psychic to know who will likely be hurt the most when the MC comes. Remember that the MC will not be a mere decline in the stock market. If my expectations are correct, then the coming MC will be pervasive, reaching into virtually every sector of the economy and society. (This holds true for European and Asian economies as well.)

---

* Kelley, E. W., Jr., Federal Reserve Board, April 28, 1998.

Who Stands to Be Hurt—and How?

In any market crash or economic contraction, the general rule is that those who are unprepared will be those who will be hurt most. But note that not all investors will be hurt. Some will actually make a profit. Before we deal with who stands to profit from a severe decline, let's see who may be hurt most.

THE RETIRED AND ELDERLY

This is the group that stands to be hurt most by a Millennium Crash. If computerized systems at the Social Security Administration break down, then these individuals will not get their checks. Since many live from check to check, there is real concern that they will not be able to pay for rent, utility bills, food and much needed medications. While this may not seem possible, remember that Y2K problems could seriously disrupt vital services. We often fail to realize how dependent we are on the systems that are responsible for maintaining things like the water supply, electrical power, telephone service and deliveries of medicines to drug stores.

In addition to these vital services, many retirees maintain money either in banks or in mutual funds. Some have their life savings invested in pension funds. Should banks close their doors, these retirees won't be able to get much needed cash. (Furthermore, some will panic, which could affect their health.)

If the Y2K meltdown reaches severe proportions, retirees will be the group that will likely feel the pressure before the rest of the public does. The steady decline in interest rates since the early 1980s has forced many retirees to make investments that are more risky than merely collecting passbook savings from a bank or credit union. The fact is that with taxes and even a mild rate of inflation, the elderly just can't make ends meet unless they've managed to put away a handy little nest egg or are supported by their families. It is realistic to believe that any disruption in the infrastructure will hurt them most.

A crash in stocks could be devastating to many retired people. If they've placed their money into mutual funds, they'd better be certain that their fund managers have a Y2K contingency plan for their stock and cash holdings, and they'd better make certain that the machinery is in place for them to take their cash out of their mutual funds when they want to. One of the worst feelings is to know that someone is holding your money and you can't get at it when you need it.

The same holds true for money kept in banks. If a retired person needs to get cash from a bank that can't produce it because of a Y2K computer glitch, there's going to be trouble. And the trouble won't be isolated to only one bank. Although the emotional reaction to such a situation may be worse than the actual situation, in the long run damage is damage regardless of its origin.

Finally, those retirees who are now living well on pensions derived from stock purchase programs will want to be very careful during the next few years. As noted earlier, many have become paper millionaires as the stock they've accumulated for 30 years in pension plans has moved up dramatically. In the event of a severe market crash, their stocks could lose more than half their value in a matter of days or even hours. If the Y2K problem causes a chain reaction of selling, many retirees could be wiped out.

While I don't mean to alarm anyone, I do mean to warn you so that you'll be prepared. If you're holding a large amount of stock that you can sell, then you might want to lighten up your holdings, generate some cash and put the cash into a few more conservative but historically safer vehicles than cash.

INVESTORS

There are millions of investors who either make their own decisions or who rely on professional money managers to make decisions for them. Making money in the greatest bull market ever in stocks has been relatively easy. Time has made many investors right even if their stock picks were bad. The simple strategy of buy and hold or buy and buy more and buy more has paid off well to patient investors. But patience can be a double-edged sword. While patience works in long-term up markets, it can lead to severe losses for those who are unable to exit positions quickly when a true panic begins. It must be noted that the big bull market of the 1980s and 1990s has seriously spoiled investors. When markets have declined sharply, they have managed to come back strongly.

The decline from July through October 1998, for example, was a near 20 percent decline that was reversed quickly and ended in a new all-time high for the Dow Jones Industrials. Yes, traders and investors have been spoiled. They have learned that *waiting* is the best policy. They have learned that it's best *not to get out* too fast, even if the market is dropping sharply, and this strategy has served them well. However, in a major new bear market, or in a market that declines on potentially serious and real news, patience will not be a virtue, rather it will be a curse. When and if the Y2K problems hit full force, the patient investor may be hit very hard as prices plummet and do not recover quickly.

BANKS AND INSURANCE COMPANIES

These institutions could also suffer serious financial consequences as their holdings and portfolios dwindle in net asset value, which could result in a chain reaction of bankruptcies. Many mergers and acquisitions since the late 1980s have created large and slow-moving institutions. They are lugubrious and cannot act quickly enough to head off disaster. It is reported that banks are spending up to a total of $4 billion to prepare for Y2K, yet this may still not be enough. If that is true, the instability in the banking system may spill over into other areas of business and finance.

Furthermore, if insurance company portfolios are hit hard, or if Y2K problems prevent them from moving their cash and stock assets quickly, then there will be serious trouble as well. Claims will go unpaid, records may be inaccessible and regularly paid benefits to policyholders will not be so regular. Consider, too, what might happen to the already inefficient and bureaucratic system of claims processing and payments to doctors who render HMO or PPO care.

CONSUMERS

Consumers will also be affected if a Y2K crisis develops. Not only will the flow of goods be disrupted, but there may actually be shortages of goods we commonly take for granted. Fresh fruits and vegetables may be in short supply as truck and transport schedules are in a shambles due to computer problems in routing. What would happen to all those tasty foods and cut meats that require refrigeration if cooling systems fail? Some Y2K analysts and forecasters suggest stocking at least a two-week supply of food well before Y2K comes. It's difficult to say how bad things will get, or if they'll be noticed at all, but a few dollars well spent in preparation could go a long way in the event of a crisis.

BUSINESS OWNERS

Clearly, a disruption in the system of delivery of goods, commodities, electronic products and other consumer items will seriously affect business. This will cause a ripple effect throughout the economy, the severity of which will be a function of how long the disruptions last. Should Y2K problems cause a lengthy delay in the delivery of goods, then employees will be laid off and the chain reaction of economic effects will be severe and extensive. It should be noted that lost consumption is usually lost. For example, if a company loses $50,000 in business due to lack of product, it is highly unlikely to recoup the $50,000 when conditions improve.

Computer-based businesses may either do extremely well or may suffer severely depending on the nature of their business. If the computer-based business depends on communication via Internet, there may be problems even if the business itself is Y2K ready. Such giants in the business of e-commerce such as Amazon.com, who sell all their products via Internet, could suffer a complete halt to their business. Given the high level of their stock prices, any disruption in their business could cause a severe crash in all Internet-related sellers and service providers. Internet commerce has become a major world business. Millions of businesses rely on the Internet for their daily transactions and communications.

FARMERS

The history of the United States is one in which farmers seem to get the short end of the stick more often than not. In the event of a Y2K crisis, farmers will find themselves with a variety of serious problems. They may find their products such as fresh fruits and vegetables or livestock and eggs backing up due to transportation disruptions. The more creative farmers will take their goods to public markets. However, this option is not available to many producers. With the farm economy already suffering due to seriously low prices, this could be the last nail in the coffin of many producers, resulting in a chain reaction of bankruptcies.

THE POOR

Ironically, it is very likely that the poor will not suffer nearly so much as the affluent since they have much less to lose. Yet those who are living in poverty may still suffer as the systems in place for delivery of their welfare checks and/or food stamps may disrupt their lives. If such delivery systems are disrupted because of Y2K problems, the results may well be rioting and/or looting. Imagine how angry people will be if they can't get their food stamps or welfare checks. Their rage would be understandable.

How to Minimize Potential Problems

A reasonable question then is, what types of investments or businesses may be safe in the event of a Y2K crisis and/or Millennium Crash? The answers are simple enough, and based on history. Those businesses that fare well will be those that have an ample supply of goods on hand in the event supplies are disrupted. Traditionally, during times of economic crisis and/or contraction, the so-called "vice" industries do well. The foremost among these is the liquor business. I'm not suggesting here that you buy a liquor store. I am merely stating a fact based on market history. Since it is not feasible for all of us to move into businesses that are relatively safe, next best is to prepare now for problems that may occur when and if the Y2K crisis develops.

Any business that can operate without being dependent on computers will likely be relatively safe. If your business depends on the computer readiness of others, you would do well to take the following measures if you haven't already done so:

SUPPLIERS

Call your suppliers and determine if they have taken the needed steps to be Y2K ready. Don't be afraid to ask questions. The only way you'll know if the firms and/or individuals you deal with are Y2K ready is to ask. You may be surprised (and not pleasantly) by the answers you'll get. You may find replies ranging from "No, we're not ready but we're working on it" to "Yes, we're totally ready" or "What's Y2K?" If you don't get an answer that's reassuring, then take action immediately to solve the potential problem.

Make certain your banking connections are ready. This applies not only to your ability to withdraw money but also to deposit it. If your business takes in money based on electronic credit card deposits, make sure the firm that processes your transactions is Y2K ready or that they have a contingency plan in the event of Y2K problems.

In some cases you may wish to acquire a signed statement from them of Y2K readiness. While this may be a sensitive issue with some firms, you will want to have this protection in the event of legal problems resulting from Y2K disruptions.

INTERNAL CONTROLS

Prepare a contingency plan that will help you operate in the event of a computer failure in your own office(s) or business. Many operations that are now computerized can be handled manually for brief periods of time. Have a plan ready well before problems arise and make certain you and your employees are trained in the manual implementation of procedures.

Battery backup systems are strongly recommended for all telephone and computer systems. Battery backups are relatively inexpensive and should be used on an everyday basis since they will eliminate the potentially negative effects of power surges. Make certain that the backup units you use have sufficient power to run your systems for at least 12 hours or, at the very minimum, for sufficient time to back up systems and bring them down safely.

Back up all of your programs and files regularly and more frequently. Since there is a distinct possibility that the Y2K bug may cause data to be lost or misfiled, it's a good idea to back up more often than usual. Surprising as it may seem, most businesses fail to back up their files with sufficient frequency since they are confident in the reliability of their systems. Those of us who have had to live through a serious system crash are well acquainted with the value of backing up systems, data and programs.

Check all your software. Make certain that all your software is Y2K ready. If it's commercially available software, check with the manufacturer's web sites or telephone hotlines to make certain your version is Y2K bug free. If your software was custom written, you must contact the developer or consultant to fix any existing or potential problems.

Make certain that you have hard copy of all vital files. This includes the names, addresses and telephone numbers of your clients, suppliers, employees, banks, law firms, accountants, etc. In the event that the memory module of your automatic dialer fails, you'll save many hours if you have the numbers organized and available.

Obtain firm commitments from suppliers. If you plan to receive any supplies beginning in mid- to late 1999 and into early 2000, make certain your suppliers have firm commitments with you at predetermined prices. In the event of Y2K shortages some suppliers may offer their goods to the highest bidder. If you haven't gotten a firm commitment, then you'll simply be told that products are unavailable when, in fact, they're being sold to those who will pay more for them.

Stock up on vital supplies. While there are those who have gone overboard with this suggestion, I am in favor of being reasonable and conservative. I suggest having no more than one month's worth of supplies on hand. If problems cannot be resolved within a month, then the entire economic system will be in a shambles and your storehouse of supplies won't do you much good unless you have found a way to deliver them to your customers without relying on delivery systems rendered dysfunctional by Y2K.

Avoid scheduling or attending any major conferences until after the first six weeks of Y2K. Should Y2K problems surface across a broad front, there will probably be transportation-related disruptions as well as problems with meeting spaces and obtaining the goods and services required for the effective functioning of meetings. It costs money to plan meetings. You lose money if you need to cancel a meeting or if your attendance declines. All of these are possible effects of Y2K.

PREPARE YOUR EMPLOYEES

Meet with employees regularly to apprise them of any new developments or changes in the Y2K situation. If employees are prepared, they will be less likely to panic. Don't be afraid to share your knowledge with them. Remember that your business can't function without them. If they're Y2K ready in their personal and family lives, then you're likely to have a reliable and rational work force in the event of a problem.

Consider contingency plans in the event that employees cannot cash their checks due to banking disruptions. This may sound alarmist, but it's worth thinking about. While it may not be easy for your business to pay employees in cash, it may become necessary. This is certainly possible if you run a smaller business. If you decide to keep cash on hand for payroll, make sure it's stored in a safe that is not in any way dependent on computers. A good old-fashioned manual combination lock safe is best for this purpose.

You may want to suspend any employee vacations for late 1999 and into early 2000. It's entirely possible that a serious Y2K problem in the travel industry could leave key employees stranded. While I do not expect this to occur, anything is possible given the relatively unprepared state of some countries, businesses and individuals.

If you offer employees medical or health care benefits, make certain your providers are ready. It's very possible that some providers of medical care will not be able to deliver. While you can't guarantee your employees that their medical providers will be completely problem-free, an ounce of prevention here may be critical to employee health.

How to Capitalize on Y2K

If your business is fully Y2K ready, use this as a selling point to increase your customers' confidence. Let your clients know that you're Y2K ready and tell them what you've done to assure smooth functioning. This little piece of public relations could go a long way toward improving your business.

You can also capitalize on Y2K madness by using creative marketing techniques. For example, you may want to advertise a "Y2K Sale" or a "Y2K Discount Program," a "Y2K Contest" or a "Pre-Y2K Closeout Sale." Be creative. There are many angles of the Y2K phenomenon that can be used to your advantage. If you're in the computer business, you can gain additional revenues by offering Y2K products and services. This could be particularly effective if offered at a sale price or bundled with other products or services. Remember that you're not the one who created the Millennium Madness.

There are many other factors to consider; however, these will be a function of your specific business. Since not all businesses offer the same products or services, take time to evaluate your own business in light of Y2K readiness. Determine your weak points as well as your strengths. Then, take action now—don't delay. If the Y2K crisis comes, and if it's nearly as severe as some would have us believe, then computer programmers and other Y2K troubleshooters will be impossible to find. Act now to find and solve any problems. It may cost you money to be fully ready for Y2K, but it will be an investment in the future of your business.

Summary

In this chapter, I have given you numerous guidelines both for determining which groups could suffer in a Y2K crisis and how to protect your business and employees in the event of a Y2K problem. The key to surviving and indeed profiting from Y2K is preparedness, and you alone bear the responsibility for being prepared. Since you know your financial circumstances and your business better than anyone else, you must be the one to rationally evaluate your Y2K readiness. And you must also be the one to develop a contingency plan. Clearly there are four phases of this process. The first is to recognize that a problem may exist, then to diagnose the problem. The second phase is to assess your vulnerability to a decline prompted by Y2K. Third, repair any visible or diagnosed problems. The fourth aspect is to have a viable contingency plan in the event that something in your planning or repair goes awry.

YOUR FINANCIAL SURVIVAL STRATEGY

Now that you have an overview of what I expect, let's take a look at a financial survival strategy.

> He that will not apply new remedies must expect new evils; for time is the greatest innovator.
> —Sir Francis Bacon

Remember that specific financial goals of each individual are different. You will need to evaluate and adapt my suggestions to your situation. What's right for a person in his or her early 30s is not necessarily right for a retiree who lives on a pension.

Remember, too, that conditions can and will change. Based on the information I have provided, you should be able to anticipate changes and avoid panic. Be flexible and open to change. Insofar as your investments are concerned, timing will be the critical variable in all you do. Don't forget that when investor emotion and public sentiment are at extreme levels, you will be most vulnerable to the madness. This is usually the time to take opposite action from what the crowd is doing.

Some of these strategies will change as a function of changes in underlying conditions. I urge you to keep in close touch with developing situations via my Internet web site:

http://www.trade-futures.com

General Financial Preparations

Well before the arrival of Y2K, you should take the following steps:

Thoroughly assess your financial situation.   Make a list of your total assets, including such things as cash in the bank, value of your home, value of collectibles, furniture, automobiles, stocks, bonds, mutual funds, available capital in brokerage accounts, equity on insurance policies, antiques, jewelry, etc. Also list your debts. Once you have done so, keep your list up to date. Once you have prepared your list, determine how much available cash you have. Take into consideration any other sources of income when determining your cash availability, and make certain you have a good idea of your monthly cost of living.

Credit cards.   If you don't already have a list of all your credit cards, make one. This is *very important,* as you will see later. Also make certain you have the telephone number (usually toll free) of each credit card company you deal with. (The telephone number is usually listed on the back of each credit card.)

Bank accounts.   Make a list of all bank accounts, their numbers, names of contacts and pass codes if you bank electronically. If you have direct deposit accounts or direct payment accounts (that is, accounts into which money is automatically deposited for you, or from which bills are paid), you may want to close these accounts. In the event of Y2K banking problems, the fate of such transfers may be questionable. Should the situation improve or become clearer, you can always reopen such accounts.

Computer records.   Keep a printed copy of important files. Don't rely on your computer for such things as name, address and telephone number files and other essential records. We fail to realize how dependent we are on computers until we can't get the information we need.

If you use an automatic dialer on your telephone, make certain you know the actual numbers; dialers could go haywire come Y2K.

The Five-Part Millennium Strategy

Once you have prepared your list and gathered the necessary financial information, consider this five-part Y2K investment strategy.

PART 1: 20 PERCENT PRECIOUS METALS AND EQUIVALENTS

As I've discussed, this is a very important part of your strategy. Investments in precious metals have been unpopular for many years, and many investors, professionals and the public alike, feel that there is no need to own precious metals when there is little or no inflation and when political or economic crises are few and far between. This is precisely my point! In the event of a Y2K financial panic or decline, there will likely be a move to hard assets or liquid assets. In other words, there will be a mass exodus out of paper (stocks and currency) into tangibles that have underlying value such as gold, silver and platinum. While this has not always been the case, the fact remains that precious metals have a very long history of reliability as hedges against crisis. Additional aspects and considerations with regard to precious metals investments are discussed in earlier chapters.

Within the category of precious metals there are many options. The following basic categories of precious metals are available to you.

Gold, silver or platinum bullion.   Some advisors will suggest you put your money into bullion for ultimate safe keeping. I strongly disagree. Bullion holdings are not so readily sold as the more negotiable forms such as coins or medals. Frequently bullion must be reassayed (i.e., weighed and certified as to purity) before a buyer will take it from you. Hence, bullion in this form is *not* what you want.

Bullion coins.   This is one of the best ways to own gold, silver and/or platinum. There are also palladium coins. A combination of all four types is reasonable, although gold coins should be the largest part of your portfolio. Silver bullion coins are considerably cheaper but require much more room for storage. There are many different types of bullion coins. It matters little which you buy, as long as they are reasonably popular. Among those currently in vogue are:

- *Gold:* U.S. Gold Eagles, Canadian Maple Leaf, South African Krugerrands, Mexican 50 Peso, English Sovereign and Australian Koala Series
- *Platinum:* American Eagle (four different sizes ranging from 1 oz. to .1 oz.), Russian Platinum Coin Sets
- *Silver:* American Silver Eagles, Silver Bullion Bags, Silver Dollars
- *Palladium:* Australian EMU Palladium Set, Tonga Palladium Coin Sets

There are various web sites from which you can get additional information. Make certain you are dealing with a reputable coin broker, and don't forget to shop around and compare prices. There can be *big* differences. You are best off establishing a relationship with a firm that will be there for you when you want to sell your coins. Many dealers will gladly sell you coins; however, when it comes to buying them back, they may not want to deal with you, or they may offer you considerably less than the going price. Check dealers thoroughly before you buy anything from them. Remember that the key to using bullion coins as part of your protective strategy will be your ability to sell them at a fair price when you're ready to get out or when you want to raise cash.

Face-to-face or electronic?   A major consideration is whether to deal with a coin broker via Internet or face to face. I firmly believe that in the event of a Y2K problem you are much better off dealing with a broker directly rather than through any form of electronic commerce. If lines of communication are disrupted, you may not be able to get quotes on line and you may not be able to transact any sales on line. You'll want to be able to walk into your coin dealer's shop and transact business the "good old-fashioned way," face to face. (Clearly, if your goal is to avoid dependence on electronic communications and computers, stay clear of anything that relies on such transactions, particularly when planning and implementing your protective strategy.)

Key issue: Who will hold your coins?   A final but very important point is the question of who will hold your coins and how you will store them. First, I stress without any hesitation that you must keep these coins in your own possession. Why leave them with anyone else? To leave your coins in the possession of a dealer who offers to "store" them for you is to place too much confidence in the financial stability and integrity of the dealer. Furthermore, you have no way of knowing in advance when you'll need or want to sell your coins. The key to all of this is to have virtually unrestricted access to your holdings when the time comes for you to liquidate them. I am not implying here that you need to keep them all under a mattress or buried in your backyard. I do, however, strongly suggest that you choose a safe place that will be easily accessible. In the event of bank problems during a Y2K crisis, your safe-deposit box also may not be the best place for your coins. You will need to find a better place.

In fact, I recommend the use of several sites in the unlikely event that one location becomes inaccessible. In choosing a spot, make certain that it is Y2K ready or, at the very minimum, that its security system is not heavily dependent on computers. As you know, there are many private storage facilities; some offer excellent security. What you choose will depend on where you live. Take the time to thoroughly investigate the best location(s) for you.

Precious metals mining stocks.   This is a major area of precious metals investing. As of early 1999, gold mining shares have been hit hard, declining to their lowest levels in years. This is no surprise given the relationship between these markets and the stock market. Prices are considerably lower than they were in the 1980s and, at the very minimum, can be considered historically cheap. The simple fact is that gold producers cannot mine gold and sell it at a profit when prices are this low. The same is true for silver. In the long run supplies are reduced, creating a potentially explosive situation. I recommend a position in precious metals stocks as a strong hedge against a declining stock market and/or a Y2K panic. Take your time in evaluating gold stocks, since there are many to choose from. I prefer some of the "old line" stocks such as Homestake Mining and American South African (ASA).

Precious metals mutual funds.   There are many funds from which to choose. Most tend to offer the same types of services, but I urge you to take some time to research their holdings as well as their upfront and hidden costs. Here is a listing of the top funds as of December 1998.

Largest Precious Metals Funds

Vanguard Spec Gold & Prec Metals

Van Eck International Investors

Benham Gold Equities Index Fund

Fidelity Sel Pre Metals & Minerals

Franklin Gold Fund

Fidelity Select American Gold

United Services Global Resources

United Services Gold Shares

Invesco Strategic Portfolios Gold

United Services World Gold

Oppenheimer Gold & Special Minerals

Van Eck Gold Resources

Lexington Gold Fund

USAA Gold Fund

Scudder Mutual Funds Gold Fund

Lexington Strategic Investments

For most investors a mutual fund is the best way to go. As long as you have confidence in the ability of your fund to avoid Y2K problems, I encourage you to put part of your assets into several funds. You may want to take a look at the mix of metals shares that your fund buys. Pick a fund that has a diversified portfolio of investments in metal producers. Take time to call the fund and ascertain their state of Y2K readiness. Don't be afraid to talk to them. Rest assured that Y2K is on everyone's mind. Funds that are Y2K ready should be more than glad to tell you of their readiness. Get something in writing from them if you can. You may want to keep it on file in case of problems at a later date.

PART 2: 40 PERCENT CASH AND EQUIVALENTS

This 40 percent category is the simplest and the most obvious, and consists essentially of two parts. Twenty percent of your assets should be held in pure cash (i.e., bank accounts, etc.) and 20 percent in government-backed securities. Having a good amount of cash on hand will be important if and when there are disruptions in the banking system and/or the credit card processing system. Based on the lack of Y2K readiness that is painfully evident in many foreign countries, I believe that American dollars offer a relatively safe haven by comparison.

There are several reasons for suggesting a strong cash position. If and when a Y2K stock market crisis develops, those who have strong cash holdings will have the buying power necessary to get into stocks at bargain prices. Earlier, I discussed the characteristics of several previous market crashes. In each case, prices declined sharply and then recovered strongly over the next few months and years. I believe the same scenario could develop in many world stock markets should a Y2K-prompted market crash develop. With cash on hand, not only will you be protected from the negative effects of a severe decline, but you will also be in the "catbird seat" ready to accumulate shares in stocks that have declined from much higher levels. Of course, short-term timing considerations will be important in such a situation; however, as a rule of thumb, a drop of 30 percent or more from highs in a quality stock is a good indication to begin some buying.

For those investors (or rather traders) with more speculative inclinations, the best stocks to buy (with considerable risk) will be those that are the most speculative, among them many of the Internet-related issues. Remember that every bull market has its "sweetheart" stocks. When the time comes, all you'll need to do is take a look at the most favored speculative issues prior to the decline. These will likely bounce back the most. Remember that speculation in these stocks is exactly that, speculation; therefore, the rallies are apt to be very short term!

For more conservative investors, purchasing a solid mutual fund at this time will be best. Given the huge amount of cash that has been pouring into mutual funds for many years now, a decline in the stock market due to Y2K selling panics could hit some funds severely as investors liquidate their holdings. Watch for some of the best funds, even though well managed, to have problems when investors sell *en masse*. Media headlines about investor panic and mutual fund liquidation will be a key signal to begin buying with your cash reserves.

The key issue in the interim, is where to keep your cash and in what form. Note that you may want to have a little more cash in your actual possession should there be credit card processing problems. Overall, I believe that banks will be safe. Ask your bank officers about their Y2K readiness. Find out if your bank has contingency plans for dealing with Y2K problems should they develop, and get a statement of readiness in writing of you can. Also, make certain you have all hard copy (i.e., paper) documentation of your account balances, account numbers, deposits, withdrawals, etc.

Whatever bank problems do arise will probably be isolated rather than pervasive. Some Y2K experts have suggested the possibility of a run on the banks or panic withdrawals in the event of a government-declared bank holiday. I am not especially concerned about such a possibility. Nor am I concerned that banks will "lose" your money due to computer-related recordkeeping problems. As long as you have proper documentation I think you'll be protected, but do ask questions. Do your best to find out how your bank plans to deal with Y2K and determine its state of readiness. If you don't like what you hear, put your money elsewhere.

U.S. Treasury bills and Treasury bonds.   While these may offer pitifully small yields, the goal here is safety, not yield. In addition to your holdings of gold and gold-related investments, your cash should be safe in U.S. government Treasury bonds and Treasury bills. Corporate commercial paper will be less safe. Although the yield here will be considerably higher than with government-backed issues, in times of crisis their safety is questionable. Since safety is what Y2K preparedness is all about, I advise you to steer clear of any investments whose safety in a Y2K financial crisis is questionable.

There are a number of mutual funds that invest only in government-backed bonds and bills. While most of these may not have a problem, remember that by dealing with the mutual fund you are adding yet another layer of potential Y2K problems. Hence, if you're not fully convinced that your mutual fund is Y2K-crisis protected, then you're better off dealing directly with the U.S. government through the Federal Reserve banks. As a further consideration, if you buy your T-bills or T-bonds at your bank, make certain that you hold the certificates in your name.

Foreign currencies.   Some investors may want to diversify their cash holdings into different currencies for added protection. If you are one of them, I recommend converting some cash into Swiss francs. The Swiss franc is likely to be one of the more stable currencies during a Y2K crisis. Note, however, that the move to a single European currency could degrade the value of the Swiss franc. You will need to make this determination when the time comes for a switch.

Multiple benefits.   I cannot overestimate the importance of having a strong cash and cash-equivalent position during times of crisis. Having cash on hand and available will serve a variety of purposes. Not only will it give you the security of knowing that you have ready cash for purchases of necessary food and medical items (should the need arise), but it will also allow you flexibility in buying stocks, mutual funds and perhaps even real estate if and when a full-scale panic liquidation develops as a result of Y2K-related problems.

PART 3: 15 PERCENT REAL ESTATE

Your overall investment strategy should include real estate. I include your home or main residence in this category. In the event of a real estate decline prior to Y2K problems or as a result of Y2K problems, you may use some of your available cash to increase your stake in this area. If your current position is less than 15 percent of assets in real estate, be patient and wait for a decline before you move to the 15 percent level.

In the event of a Y2K market panic and possible economic decline, real estate prices may contract; however, I believe that your main real estate holding—your home—should be safe and should be held. If you currently own real estate that has shown strong growth over the last few years, then I would consider decreasing your holdings in favor of a stronger cash position. This is particularly true in rental properties. Should a Y2K decline result in a period of economic contraction and a subsequent increase in unemployment, you may experience some problems with rental properties. If a decline develops, you can use your strong cash position to buy distressed properties when the time is right.

Note: I do not purport to be a real estate expert. My comments here are based on the possibility of a rather obvious scenario. If you have expertise in real estate, then use your best judgment; however, take into consideration the possible effects of an economic contraction based on Y2K-related problems.

PART 4: 15 PERCENT COLLECTIBLES

This area includes such things as art, antiques, precious stones, rare coins (which would also have precious metals value), rare books, antique rugs and tapestries, musical instruments, folk art, and so on. Collectibles have increased substantially in value over the years. They will likely continue to do so. Hence, they offer solid long-term growth potential as well as good protection in the event of a Y2K decline. Certainly storage and insurance are considerations. In the event of a Y2K crisis you may find many valuable collectibles on the auction block. Your ready reserve of cash will help you here as well.

Note: Unless you are an expert, however, be certain to do business only with reputable dealers.

PART 5: 10 PERCENT IN STOCKS

I suggest reducing your stock market holdings (other than investments in precious metals) to about 10 percent. These actions should be taken well in advance of year-end 1999. You do not need to sell your holdings all at once to get to this point. Some of you may want to sell off less than that amount. This is understandable, particularly if the market has served you well over the years. I can only sound a strong note of caution to you. Stock market speculators will use any and all excuses to generate excitement and volatility. The Y2K situation is one of the best excuses ever for a market sell-off of considerable proportion. I do not believe that the market will escape unscathed. To protect yourself, I strongly suggest you reduce holdings in stocks. Yes, I may be totally wrong and you will lose out on additional gains. However, if I'm right, then you may do more than save money; you may also save yourself from financial ruin.

Those who are more experienced in the market may want to take more aggressive actions in the form of short selling, writing naked calls, buying puts or selling covered call options. The most aggressive and speculative traders will want to consider futures and futures options. Although this book is not about market timing, I can offer you a number of suggestions about some things to watch for:

- Record high trading volume and mass speculative buying of stocks are an indication that a top is near.
- An exceptionally high level of optimism among the public is a good sign that all is not well. The general public is usually wrong at important market turning points. Monitor public sentiment to see just how optimistic investors are about the U.S. economy.
- Closely watch the Y2K situation beginning in the summer of 1999. See how stocks react to possible problems in the investment sector. This will give you a good idea of how the market may react when the real crisis hits.

When you sell stocks, do so on a scale up. Sell on good news. If the current stock market follows the pattern of other speculative markets, then the most speculative leg of the bull move is yet to come. Take advantage of this speculative bubble to lighten up your holdings.

Summary

Preparation will be your key to survival in the event of a Y2K market and economy panic. Cash and your ability to access it will be the fuel you will need to not only survive a panic but to profit from it as well. While your individual situation will vary according to your earnings, age and financial goals, use what I have told you as an important guideline in planning. I cannot stress too strongly how important and necessary it is to plan well in advance. If my expectations are wrong, if Y2K comes and goes without incident, then you will have been prepared. Sometimes insurance is necessary and we must pay the price for that insurance. Facing what may be the most important crisis in many years, insurance is more than just a good idea—it's a necessity!

PERSONAL PREPAREDNESS

There are many ways to protect yourself. What you do depends on what you are

> While we are postponing, life speeds by.
>
> —Seneca

seeking to protect. In this chapter, I will provide advice for each major category. While I may not be able to cover each and every detail, I believe you'll get the general idea. (You may also want to check some of the resources listed later in this book.) Remember that there will always be the temptation to go overboard and panic. I urge you, above all, not to panic.

Home and Personal Property

It is unlikely that you will need to be concerned about your home or your personal property if you are Y2K ready. Some alarmists would have you believe that Y2K problems will be so severe that there will be rioting and looting. Some have gone so far as to suggest that you are best off selling your home and belongings, and taking your family— along with food, medical supplies, weapons, ammunition and electrical generating equipment—into the back woods far from civilization.

I do not subscribe to this point of view. The odds are that things won't get anywhere close to the crisis point insofar as civil unrest is concerned.

Those of us who can maintain a rational and reasonable approach to Y2K may want to consider the following safeguards:

▪ Make sure your property insurance premiums are paid up and your policies are active. You may want to prepay a few months' insurance premiums (if you pay monthly) to make sure that you are fully covered and up-to-date for both fire and theft. Some of you may need up-to-date appraisals for valuables, complete with photographs. Take care of these as soon as possible. Whether there are serious Y2K threats to home and property or not, these items should be updated regularly.

▪ Make certain that your home security system is Y2K ready. If there is civil unrest, it will be important that your security system is fully functional and unlikely to malfunction due to Y2K glitches.

▪ Check your heating and/or air conditioning systems to be sure they are Y2K ready. If they're not, the system may not operate properly.

▪ Secure a backup electrical system if you're concerned about your utility provider. This is especially crucial if someone in your home must have electrical power for health reasons. There are many power generators available at reasonable prices.

▪ Have some food on hand. Some Y2K experts have suggested that supplies of food may be disrupted. I have my doubts about how serious this will be (if it happens at all). If you are concerned, it might be reasonable to have 2 to 4 weeks' supply of nonperishable food on hand.

▪ Have a cell phone handy and charged, and keep a few backup batteries ready. Some respected authorities claim that telephone service may be disrupted. I also have my doubts about how serious this may get. While traditional wired service may experience some problems, it is unlikely that cell phones will. This system is more up-to-date and was probably designed with Y2K in mind. You might also want to investigate connecting your cell phone to a modem line in the event your telephone system fails.

▪ If you rent, ask your property owner about Y2K preparedness. If the building is not Y2K ready, there may be heating problems and even problems with building entry and exit, parking garage, etc. These may seem like small concerns, but they can add up to big problems.

Note: If you run a business out of your home, then you might want to take the precautions outlined for business owners earlier in this chapter.

Health

What can you do to avoid health problems in the event of a Y2K crisis? Clearly what you do will depend on how serious you believe the situation will be. I do not believe that Y2K is going to cause serious health care disruptions, but there are a number of things you can do to prepare. How far you go with these suggestions is up to you, of course, but I reiterate that reason, not panic, should guide your decisions.

- *Stockpile medications that are vital to your health,* such as life-saving drugs for your heart, high blood pressure, diabetes, convulsive disorders and the like. I see no reason to store more than several months' supply. Some forecasters claim that the manufacture and distribution of medications could be disrupted. In this case, a little foresight and a few dollars spent on prevention could be worth their weight in gold. If some medications are in short supply, they may be rationed or prices may be high. (I include in this category things such as oxygen, medicated ointments, antibiotics, etc.)

- *Have some bottled water on hand.* There are many sources for water; however, your local supplier of bottled water is the best place to buy it. Plan on six glasses per person per day plus some for cooking.

- *Get a complete physical well before the end of 1999.* If you have undiagnosed or lingering health problems, you'll want to make certain that you are either cured or in treatment well before early millennium problems develop in health care delivery.

- *Avoid scheduling elective surgery* starting in late 1999 until several months into the Year 2000 just in case there are problems.

MISCELLANEOUS PERSONAL PRECAUTIONS

- Avoid airplanes on the last day of this millennium and on the first few days of the next millennium. I don't consider this to be an unreasonable warning. From all I've read, it's possible that there may be some problems with scheduling and possibly with the most crucial issue, air traffic control. If you don't have to be on a plane or train at that time, then avoid it.

- Stay off the road. If traffic signals fail, then you'd best not be in a car. There are reasonable doubts about whether many cities in the United States are Y2K ready. If traffic lights aren't operating correctly, it could result in numerous accidents. I recommend particular caution on the night of December 31, 1999.

Avoiding Fear and Panic

When we think of fear, we rarely attach it to such things as bankruptcy, loss of money, financial consequences or a "run" on the banks. Fear is commonly reserved for more tangible or direct threats, such as the threat of crime, impending failure or perhaps an auto or airplane accident. Yet fear of the unknown is more pervasive than any of us care to admit. Concern about a plethora of problems that *might* occur when Y2K approaches is a powerful stimulus. As this book is being written, the media have not yet started a major publicity campaign about Y2K but it is surely coming. Logic and preparation will help alleviate fear and prevent the kind of reaction that could cause a few simple Y2K problems to snowball into a landslide of panic. Logic and preparation will be your greatest assets in the event of a Y2K crisis, no matter how small or large it may be.

It is frequently the anticipation of negative consequence that leads to fear. Fear results in behaviors that may not necessarily be appropriate to the situation. In other words, there are rational fears and irrational fears. The soldier in the battlefield, for example, may flee or fight in response to fear. In that case, fear mobilizes the defensive processes and may lead to beneficial, life-saving action. However, in less obvious situations, when the threat is not clearly known, the resulting defensive behavior may not be appropriate to the situation.

Consider the plight of the investor who responds to the fear of financial loss. Assume that he or she has invested in a given stock and that, shortly thereafter, stock prices begin to decline on a broad front. The investor hears that stocks are declining sharply; in fact, the news is very negative indeed. The decline now taking place is one of the worst on record. This scenario is not unlike the one you may have to face when and if Y2K problems develop in the financial markets. Investors fearing a decline will sell their stocks, which in turn, will cause others to sell and the chain reaction will continue. What to do?

Clearly, there are several possible courses of action. The *logical response* to this perceived threat is to do nothing. Often, the best response is to sit tight and let the selling take its course. Frequently the end result is a return to rational behavior and a recovery in the market.

What is perhaps more important: Logic would have dictated, in advance, what action, if any, the investor should have taken *before* the event occurred. In other words, *preparedness* is a key factor. In the case of Y2K, preparation will cause the investor either to liquidate stock investments well in advance of a Y2K-prompted market decline or to substantially lighten up his or her holdings. The investor would also have placed protective stop loss orders with the broker. Another alternative would be to place some or all of the funds into protected investments. Regardless of which action you choose, they should be taken *in advance of* the market decline. Preparation in anticipation of such events and rational planning will save you from potentially irrational behavior(s) that may be the result of fear.

Summary

In this chapter, I provided specific guidelines to help you prepare for whatever problems the approach of the Year 2000 may bring. Exact strategies will vary depending on your individual circumstances. Use the guidelines in this chapter to develop your own strategy, and remember that a plan is useless unless it is implemented.

PANICS, PANDEMONIUM AND PROFITS

$\mathbf{I}$t has been said that change equals opportunity. Where great fear and panic

Fear makes men believe the worst.
—Quintis Rufus: Alexander the Great

exist, great opportunity for profit exists. Throughout history we see countless examples of how large armies have been defeated by smaller, weaker adversaries who employed fear as their main weapon; how investor panic precipitated major market crashes; how fear of the unknown dissuaded the advance of reason and science; and how fear of self has inhibited true greatness in personal growth. Fear of fear is perhaps our greatest enemy. Yet fear is the greatest asset of the logical, savvy, calculating Machiavellian investor. Fear is at the root of most investor and trader losses and it is the stock and trade of many professional traders.

More than ever before we are in a time period where fear may be the key ingredient to a stock market and economic volatility never before seen. The myth, madness, prophecy and technological nightmare that await us in the Year 2000, when combined with fear and the human propensity for irrational behavior in the face of fear, may all combine to create one of the most severe economic conflagrations ever witnessed. Will the coming collapse be a lengthy one or merely a brief syncope that destroys millions of investors in its wake and creates unprecedented opportunities for a relative handful of others?

Is it possible that there will be no collapse at all? Could it be that the anticipation will be worse than the reality? Will all the gnashing of teeth and all the warnings amount to nothing more than a tempest in a teapot? Will the expectation be the sound and fury, in fact signifying nothing? Time will tell, but history will teach. Let's examine a few selected "major" incidents in U.S. stock market history since the 1950s to see if there are any parallels. I'm certain that even before I begin to show you some of the similarities between what has been and what's to come, you'll say to yourself "there can be no comparison because there has never been anything like this before." I respectfully submit to you that each of the incidents I am about to discuss was seen in the same way as it was happening.

Sputnik I—Eye in the Sky Decline

Human nature is predictable and, in retrospect, often humorous. When we look back at events that seemed important, we often laugh at how silly we were to attach so much significance to them. Consider the space race of the 1950s as an example. On October 4, 1957 the Russians demonstrated their superiority in the space race by launching *Sputnik I*. The launching took many people by surprise. It was clear that the Russians were technologically superior to the United States and now they had an awesome new spy device as well as a means for dropping nuclear missiles on us. The resulting panic not only by the U.S. public but also by the United States government, military and CIA prompted not only a decline in stock prices but also a commitment by the U.S. government to ultimately spend billions of dollars to achieve superiority in space.

Figure 12.1 shows the "*Sputnik I* Decline" and its aftermath in terms of stock prices. As you can see, the market started its decline before the launch of *Sputnik* and then made its low not too long thereafter. Prices then began a slow and very steady move up that lasted many months. This example demonstrates how investor panic tends to be negated by reality. Those who panicked sold stocks and lost money while those who were rational bought stocks and fared well indeed. It is interesting

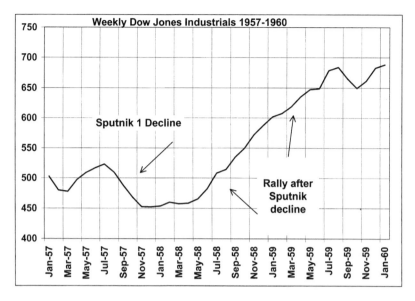

FIGURE 12.1   **Weekly Dow Jones Industrials 1957–1960, Showing Effect of** *Sputnik 1*

to note that the launch of *Sputnik I* and the anxiety it created came very close to the bottom of an existing decline. Most often we find that negative news creates the panic that tends to make the low.

The Cuban Missile Crisis

Perhaps younger readers may not remember the Cuban Missile Crisis of the 1960s. I urge you to heed this historical example. I think you will find, as I do, that history does repeat itself. Knowing its lessons and making use of the knowledge is what will not only save us, but will help us profit.

In October 1962, U.S. President John F. Kennedy was informed by military advisors that Fidel Castro of Cuba had installed Russian-supplied missiles on his island. Reconnaissance confirmed that these missiles were present and that they could, within minutes, deliver a crippling nuclear attack on key cities in the United States. Kennedy demanded removal of the missiles. The Russians refused. Over a period of seven emotion-filled days, Kennedy decided to deploy a naval blockade of Cuba in order to cut the island off from receiving further Russian weapons and supplies needed to arm the missiles. A major confrontation developed between the United States and Russia. Many investors feared that there would be a full-scale nuclear war. As a result, the stock market declined sharply.

The market had already been declining from its 1961 peak when the news came. Hence, the negative news that caused a further decline merely added to an already negative sentiment among investors, providing additional fuel for their negative attitudes. Figure 12.2 shows this decline and its aftermath. As you can see, the decline proved to be a fantastic buying opportunity. Prices rose steadily for several years after the crisis. Panic provided an opportunity for highly emotional investors to get burned while it provided an opportunity for savvy professionals to load up on stock and make money.

In the end, the market regained its losses quickly as stocks soared following a resolution of the crisis. Those investors who had panicked lost large amounts of money while those who were logical and stayed their ground or exited stocks very early fared well. Those who actually profited were those who had the emotional control and foresight to buy stocks as prices declined due to investor panic. The lessons are

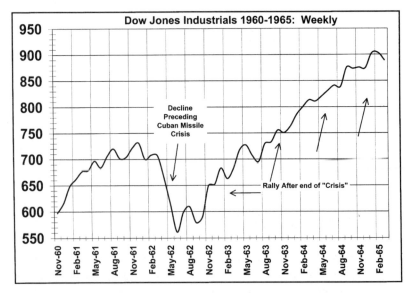

FIGURE 12.2   **Weekly Dow Jones Industrials 1960–1965, Showing Effect of Cuban Missile Crisis**

clear, and I believe they are applicable not only to most declines in the market but to a potential Y2K market collapse as well.

The Market Crash of 1987: Fear and Fact

A similar panic gripped the U.S. stock markets in October of 1987. Known as Black Monday, the U.S. stock market fell over 22 percent on October 19, 1987. This decline was about twice the size of the October 29, 1929 stock market crash. Over $500 billion in paper stock profits were wiped out. Traders, professionals and the public panicked in a chain reaction that sent stocks plummeting. In retrospect, a few things are quite clear and have direct bearing on what may soon come to pass. Following the Crash of 1987, the stock market regained its strength and went on to score new all-time highs. Those who panicked were losers. Those who kept their wits about them survived. Those who had a contingency plan and knew what to do made money. Several facts are paramount and must be kept in mind if and when a market crash comes in connection with Y2K crises.

The lack of accurate information was a key factor in exacerbating the decline and in leading to more panic. If you wanted to know the current price of your stocks, you were out of luck. This was caused by the failure of electronic monitoring systems to keep pace with the speed of transactions. In the event of a market decline precipitated by Y2K problems, the same situation may develop. When the rest of the world is selling in a panic, your best bet will be to sit tight, secure in the knowledge that you have prepared well in advance. Figure 12.3 is a good illustration of what happened. As you can see, the Crash of 1987 was severe and fast, yet following the decline prices slowly but surely started their upward trend and continued higher until the 1987 peak was surpassed. Investors who bought into the 1987 decline fared well.

The Bear Market of 1998

The Dow Jones Industrial Average made an all-time peak in mid-July 1998. At first the peak was a minor one; however, it soon gained negative momentum, eventually culminating in four days of panic in late August. As you can see, the market made a low and then—following a

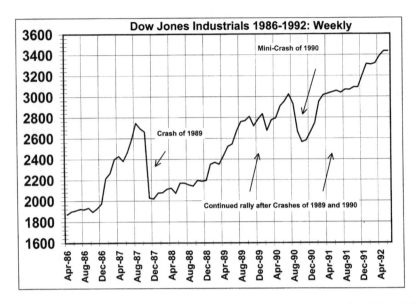

FIGURE 12.3   **Weekly Dow Jones Industrials 1986–1992, Showing Effect of the Crash of 1989 and the Mini Crash of 1990**

period of consolidation—moved steadily and persistently higher to make a new all-time high in late November. During the period of declining prices, the public and the professionals were highly negative about the future of the market. Still, the market climbed a "wall of worry," eventually reaching a new all-time high. As in the cases cited above, investors who panicked in August sold near the low, while those who had a plan to buy, and followed their plan, fared well.

A Hypothetical Y2K Market Scenario

Imagine, if you will, the following scenario. It is presented as an example only. The dates *do not* constitute an actual forecast; they are part of an entirely hypothetical scenario.

THE SETTING

By early October 1999 the U.S. stock market, along with many stock markets throughout the world, are still strong after attaining new all-time highs. The outlook for business and the economy are healthy. Inflation is growing at an acceptable rate and the U.S. Federal Reserve has taken no action to raise rates. In fact, they have held rates reasonably low. Corporate earnings are holding well, and the international situation is reasonably peaceful (other than the usual demons).

Investors are optimistic and seemingly prepared for any "reasonable" market decline. There are some concerns about Y2K problems; however, they are not nearly so serious as many have predicted. In fact, Y2K has been somewhat of a Godsend since billions upon billions have been spent on Y2K readiness. In fact, the money spent substantially benefitted the U.S. economy.

THE PANIC

At the end of the first week of October 1999 a major U.S. bank announces that it has discovered a serious Y2K-related problem caused by an out-of-date computer chip in some of their processing systems. They are concerned that it will take at least five months for their operations to return to normal, and they cannot guarantee the accuracy of account balances, deposits and funds. At about the same time, several banks in Japan and South America announce similar problems. Shares of their stock begin to decline sharply as those with accounts at these banks begin to withdraw their funds quickly via wire transfers. A chain reaction caused by fear ripples through the banking industry.

Government officials in several countries come forward with announcements that their systems are not Y2K ready although they had previously announced 95 percent readiness. There are concerns that the U.S. government will not be able to send out Social Security checks or pay military salaries and government employee paychecks for up to six weeks. This is considered serious, since it is estimated that about 30 percent of the U.S. population is in one way or another adversely affected by this situation.

Fearing an even worse impact, government employees, retirees and military employees flock to their banks to withdraw money they will need in order to get through six weeks or more without pay. The evening news shows lines of people waiting at their banks to withdraw funds. The news is compelling and arouses fear in millions of people. Their reaction is to rush to the bank and withdraw money, or to rush to stores and stockpile food "before it is all gone." They panic because "everyone else is doing it." Still others begin to liquidate stocks across a broad front, exacerbating the decline, which feeds on itself and causes even more selling.

The U.S. president declares a state of emergency and addresses the nation on radio and television; however, his words do little to calm the people.

THE LULL

Reports that they may not be fully ready for Y2K begin to crop up from all sectors of business. However, efforts are doubled and tripled and calm soon returns.

The stock market surges back up as nervous investors breathe a sign of relief. Few realize that this may be merely a precursor, a dress rehearsal for what could still come in early 2000. Few remember that declines of this type are fairly typical during the month of October. (Most investors are unaware that stock prices tend to follow a seasonal pattern.)

Those who panicked and sold their stocks during the decline have lost a considerable amount of money. Savvy investors who bought into the decline have done well indeed.

The preliminary panic serves as a warning of what is yet to come. Many have been burned because they reacted emotionally. Some have learned from it, but most have not. When the next crisis hits they will again react with fear because they are unprepared.

LOGIC AND PREPARATION VERSUS FEAR AND HOPE

The illogical response to this hypothetical situation is panic liquidation. When panic grips many investors at the same time, market behavior is exaggerated and magnified. Groundless fear is worse than fear caused by real situations. The consequence of panic liquidation is a market decline much worse than might have been the case had there been reasonable preparation and planning in anticipation of a possibly severe market decline.

Things may not happen in a way that resembles my hypothetical situation. In fact, they may happen at a different time; or they may begin from much lower levels in the stock market. Regardless of what actually happens, you will be ready to capitalize on it *if* you have prepared. This is a truism; it is reasonable and rational. It makes sense and it's intelligent. But who said that all investors are rational and intelligent? *You* can be.

"THIS TIME THINGS WILL BE DIFFERENT"

Investors are notorious for finding excuses, rationalizations and intellectualizations. Even after reading this book, after reviewing the repetitive nature of history and understanding the cyclical patterns in markets, some investors will fool themselves into thinking that this time things will be different. Here are some of the excuses you may already be hearing:

■ "The Y2K stock market crash will be the worst in history because we have never encountered this type of problem before."

■ "When the market declines this time, it won't recover like it has done so often in the past because this crash will involve all markets in the world."

■ "There is no cure or fix for the Y2K problem; therefore, the market will decline and not recover."

■ "Banks, governments and money managers aren't ready for Y2K. The crash this time will be one that engulfs all major institutions and therefore it will be the biggest crash ever, one from which it will take years to recover."

■ "The stock market has been up for too long and it has gone up too far without a breather. The Y2K situation is the perfect set up for a top and a full-scale economic depression."

■ "Although the United States is almost Y2K ready, other countries are not, and they're the weakest link in the chain. This will cause markets to crash and the U.S. market cannot remain immune to the chain reaction."

These are just a few of the many excuses you'll hear when the time approaches. There will be a litany of "this time it's for real." And it may very well be for "real." The question is not so much whether there will be some sort of financial reaction but rather how long will it last, how will we prepare for it so we will be protected, and how can we profit from it. Admittedly the last question is a mercenary one, but aren't we all interested in profit? If the profit can come from using good judgment, shouldn't we strive for that profit?

An Overview

Based on my view of stock market history, here are some things to consider:

1. *Major stock market declines have, for the most part, taken place during the declining phase* of either the approximate nine-year or four-year cycle. The Year 2000 is a potentially critical time frame since I place the last low as having been made in 1998.

2. *Stock market "crashes" have most often been severely overdone* by panic reactions of investors.

3. *Most stock market crashes and severe declines have resulted from over-speculation* and blatant investor disregard of negative economic and fundamental considerations. One can reasonably say that the U.S. stock market since the mid-1990s has been a highly speculative game wherein the stock of totally worthless companies has risen, in some cases, by several hundred percent. Hence, the market has set itself up for a fall.

4. *Stock investments in traditional companies (i.e., medical, electronic, industrial) should constitute only a given percentage of your assets.* Even if you are more heavily invested in stocks than in other areas, you will know when to lighten your portfolio if you heed the clear warnings, among them rampant speculation, stock market cycles and economic cycles. Your investments should ideally be spread across a number of different areas, including precious metals.

5. *Most, perhaps all, severe market declines signal trouble* for a considerable period of time prior to the event. I do not believe that a Y2K-inspired market decline will come out of "nowhere." There will be plenty of warning and, therefore, plenty of time for you to prepare.

6. *Few markets decline severely without a respite or upside correction.* Therefore, liquidation of stocks in response to fear is

likely to be an incorrect response inasmuch as fear will likely not set in at its greatest level until the worst is about over. Selling will be at its worst close to the bottom. Markets that decline can rally sharply, giving those who want to exit a better place to sell than panic-selling at the bottom.

The lessons to be learned are:

1. *Fear is an emotional response to either real or imagined threats.* If fear is the motivating factor in response to an imagined situation or to imagined consequences of a situation, then the resultant behavior will, a great majority of the time, be inappropriate and lead to undesirable results. Panic and fear will be in good supply come Y2K. I urge you to prepare for the fear so you do not become another statistical casualty of panic.

2. *Preparation, planning, logical anticipation and discipline* are actions and behaviors that will limit or entirely eliminate the illogical responses that tend to characterize the fear response.

3. *The lessons of economic history, though by no means totally perfect* or 100 percent applicable to every situation, are important guidelines to future behavior and planning. The lessons can be learned, and those who are intent on planning ahead must study economic history, cycles and market history.

4. *Economic cycles and market patterns are fairly obvious to students of market behavior.* Although they are neither perfect nor 100 percent reliable, they are sufficiently predictable to permit planning and development of a general investment "road map" or timetable.

Clearly, then, the way to avoid the potentially destructive consequences of fear as we approach and enter Y2K is to be prepared, to combat fear with logic and to replace emotional response with intelligent and well-planned programs.

PANIC

Panic is a form of fear. Economic panics and panics in response to perceived economic threats are no less destructive than panics in response to other potential or real threats. When someone yells "Fire" in a crowded theater and virtually all of the terrified patrons rush to the same exit, the result will most certainly be death and destruction. Economic panics are no different. There have been literally hundreds of panics in the history of world economics. Without too much thought we can remember such panics as the 1929 and 1987 stock market crashes, as well as the banking panics during the 1930s' economic decline. History has clearly shown that panics are the worst form of fear.

Although varying levels of fear may be experienced at any one time, only the most intense and pervasive fear leads to panic. History also teaches that panics have more often than not been witnessed during the declining phases of long-wave economic cycles and during the declining portion of shorter market cycles. The ideal or most logical way to cope with panic is to act in a fashion that will either minimize its impact on your finances or that will entirely avoid its negative consequences.

Remember also that financial panics (whether real or in response to perceived threats) are not necessarily only related to bear markets or to the declining phase of long-term cycles. Although clearly less obvious, buying panics can also develop during the rising portion of economic cycles and trends. The fear that a given investment, buying opportunity, home, stock or food will be in short supply can drive prices to dizzying heights. This has happened many times throughout the course of history. This could well be the case if a Y2K panic takes hold. The effects of fear could be far worse than any actual Y2K series of events.

Buying and selling panics are no strangers to economic history. They take the form of such events as the Tulip Mania, the South Sea Bubble, Sutter's Folly or the rampant speculation that has accompanied most stock market peaks. Buying panics develop more slowly and are more obvious to the informed investor earlier in their inception than are selling panics. Regardless of whether panics are subtle, obvious, inspired by news or inspired by rumor, their negative consequences are, for the most part, avoidable. Y2K is merely another notch in the belt of history.

DENIAL

Psychiatry and psychology have long recognized the role of defense mechanisms in human behavior. When the impact or perceived impact of certain events or experiences is too difficult to cope with, the mind may opt to deny or minimize the reality. An investor may place funds with a money manager who fails to perform well. Perhaps 20 percent of the initial equity may be lost, yet the investor ignores the poor performance, fails to analyze the losses and continues to believe that success will come. Denial may also be operating in the case of those who are unwilling to admit that there may be problems in Y2K. In spite of clear evidence that Y2K problems exist and may bring many systems, governments and markets to a standstill, denial is what keeps people from preparing. Denial results in a failure to plan ahead.

Consider the following situation: You read this book and decide to prepare your investment portfolio by accumulating some gold-mining stocks. Your investment begins to deteriorate. It appears that the company whose shares you have decided to buy is losing money because of a weak cash market for gold. Your technical indicators have turned negative. The news is negative. The Y2K problems that were expected fail to materialize. You decided in advance that you would liquidate and take your loss at a certain point. Your investment has reached that point, yet you fail to follow through. You sway from your plan. You deny the reality of the situation, deciding instead to "give it one more day." "One day" becomes several weeks. You are still holding your "investment." Once again you have altered your plan, lost your discipline and denied the reality of your situation. Why? Because you feared taking the loss.

On the other hand, consider the opposite scenario. You prepare for Y2K by accumulating, among other things, gold shares. The Y2K situation begins to develop and fear dominates the markets. Your gold shares soar. At the first large move up you deviate from your plan and sell out. The market moves several hundred percent higher. What caused you to sway from your plan? Among other emotions it was the fear that prices had reached their peak and the denial that things could get worse. You failed because you reacted emotionally, not logically.

Denial is perhaps the single most pervasive factor in the investment world. Almost every one of us has, at one time or another, fallen victim to denial in speculation and/or investing. What are the mechanisms and motivations that govern the use of this defense mechanism? Here are some ideas for you to consider:

1. *Unwillingness to accept a loss causes us to deny the existence or importance of that loss,* and we open the door to further losses and further breaches of discipline.

2. *Accepting a loss is ego deflating.* By denying the importance of a loss or by negating its existence, we "save" our ego from having to face the reality of the situation. We feel, subconsciously, that everything is well when, in fact, our rational mind knows that all is not well.

3. *By denying a situation indefinitely, we need not deal with it.* This is an approach used all too often in everyday life. Procrastination is a way of denying the importance of events and required actions.

4. *Denial is not reality based.* Denial constitutes a regression to techniques we may have used when we were very young. The fact that denial may have worked for us in our childhood makes us believe (mistakenly) that it will work for us as adults.

5. *Denial leads to more denial, and more denial leads to more mistakes.* It can only, therefore, lead us to losses or to inappropriate decisions insofar as investments are concerned.

6. *Denial has no place in the investor's repertoire.* While denial can be valuable in day-to-day emotional life, for limited periods of time or for brief periods during extreme crisis, it is counterproductive when used in place of decisive action.

If and when the economic events I am expecting come to pass, investors, politicians and economists will all be inclined to avoid dealing with the painful realities. When and if stock prices crash due to Y2K problems, investors will deny the growing cataclysm. They will tell themselves that the worst is almost over. By denying the warnings, which will be clear and unmistakable prior to the next severe decline, investors will find themselves in a worse situation than if they had accepted the reality when it was there for the seeing. They won't be alone. Denial will be rampant in virtually every sector of the economy, whether in the banking industry, in the business world or in monetary policy. To avoid the serious consequences of denial, I suggest the following:

1. *Come to terms with your own psychology.* Think about times in your life, past and present, in which you have used denial as a defense. Has it served you well? Did denying reality make things better for you, or did it make things worse?

2. *Avoid procrastination.* Procrastination is a form of denial. Do you let your investments take care of themselves? Do you procrastinate in spite of knowledge that suggests specific action? If so, analyze your behavior and take steps to change it.

3. *Avoid denial through planning and organization.* Although there is no guarantee that organization, direction, planning and systematic preparation will eliminate denial, they will facilitate action and minimize the possibility that denial will interfere with your behavior.

4. *Get a partner.* Two heads may be better than one when it comes to denial. A partner may help you admit to things that you won't or can't see.

5. *Plan well ahead of time.* If you act before pain has set in, there will be nothing to avoid deny.

6. *Accept the reality of your financial situation.* Avoid delusions, fantasies and/or unrealistic expectations. Know where you stand and evaluate your situation regularly. By doing so, you will limit the possibility of denial creeping into your behavior.

In short, logic, preparation, acceptance of reality, realistic expectations about the future and the avoidance of unrealistic expectations will help you deter the potentially serious consequences of denial. In the dark days ahead, those who continue to deny the seriousness of reality will be those who are first felled by its arrows. Denial has been the *modus operandi* of governments throughout the world for many years.

Regardless of ideology—communist, socialist or capitalist—governments throughout the world have denied the existence of basic economic principles, long-wave economic cycles, the needs of their people and the importance of sane economic policies. The bitter fruits of their denial have come back to haunt them. The collapse of the Soviet Union, for example, was a clear case of denial. Still another terrible harvest may soon be upon us, this time wearing the disguise of Y2K. Denial of its ultimate reality can only make the final situation worse than it might have been if dealt with appropriately and within a reasonable amount of time.

INTELLECTUALIZATION

A more subtle form of defensive behavior on the part of the investor is "intellectualization." By using what is believed to be logic, reason and rational evidence, the investor attempts to justify a given situation intellectually. Although the logic may be correct, and although theoretically a given position should lead to given conditions, reality may not coincide with theory. Those who practice this form of defensive behavior are avoiding reality by taking refuge in what should be, not in what is. Intellectualization is running rampant with regard to the Y2K situation. There are experts everywhere. Some are thinking the situation away while others are thinking the situation into crisis.

There is no doubt that markets are frequently predictable and logical; however, anyone who has had even the slightest exposure to the markets knows that there are times when logic and intellectual considerations do not play an important role. There are clearly times when emotion takes over and intelligence fails.

When panic, greed and emotion dominate a market, the logic of earnings, price/earnings (PE) ratios, fundamentals and chart patterns go out the window. Replaced by fear, poor judgment and irrational behavior, intellectual considerations have little effect. Yet, there are those who sit and watch the reality of the marketplace, taking solace in the intellectual facts and figures. Their thoughts might be as follows: "The charts and statistics indicate that this price decline was not supposed to happen. I'll just hold on until things go the way they should." They ignore their own risk-limiting rules.

An example of intellectualization as it relates to the Y2K situation is an analysis that rests its case on the logic of certain events happening in sequence. This approach ignores the wild card—investor fear and panic. The intelligent approach to solving a technological approach of this magnitude can only take us so far. To look at solutions to Y2K problems from a technical standpoint and to then say that problems will be minimal due to "fixes" in software and/or hardware is irrational. The lowest common denominator is the person or people who panic. Their behavior must be given major consideration in developing a possible Y2K scenario.

A purely logical line of reasoning might be acceptable from a scientific point of view, but the fact is that the economy, the markets and price trends are not totally scientific. Although in the long run the laws of supply and demand may reign supreme, prices may deviate from the ideal for extended periods of time. To cling tenaciously to ideal expectations, to explain away reality with intellectual excuses, is just another form of denying what is real.

Many people hold scientific reasoning, logic and "intelligent" behavior in high esteem. Although these qualities may serve us well in the business world, they may actually prove counterproductive when quick response and quick decision making are required. The clear thinking, logical business-school graduate may find his or her logic useless during panics. In fact, to take intellectual refuge in "what should be" may result in financial ruin. I believe that Y2K problems will test this type of reasoning to its limit. Although it is correct to practice emotional control and self-discipline, it can be financially disastrous to use intellectual arguments to support an obviously incorrect and illogical position in one's investments.

PSYCHOLOGICAL PREPARATION

Each individual has different needs, wants and emotional makeup. We understand, interpret and respond to similar situations in different ways. Inasmuch as we have distinctly different responses and coping styles, no single solution or set of rules will be sufficient to prepare all of us emotionally for the economic crises I've described in this book. There are, however, a number of general considerations and guidelines that can help point you in the right direction. When and if the MC reaches severe proportions, you will do well if you are prepared psychologically as well as financially. Here, for your analysis and consideration, are a number of suggestions derived from my understanding of human psychology, market history and the Y2K problem.

1. Prepare well ahead of time.   This will help you avoid the errors that tend to occur when you respond with emotion. If you accept my conclusion that the Crash of 1987, the Cuban Missile Crisis and the Crash of 1989 were examples of how being prepared can help you survive and prosper, then you must plan ahead. In order to do this, you will need to be deliberate about what stocks you own, how long you own them, how and when you liquidate, and if and when you want to be on the short side of stocks. It's probably better to be a bit too early than a bit too late. To act once the Y2K crisis has hit is not to *act,* it is to *react.*

2. Keep in close touch with your financial situation.   Know where you stand financially. If you know your situation, you'll avoid acting without knowledge. Preparing for Y2K would be a great way to get in touch with your situation. When and if fear and panic grip the financial markets, you'll be less likely to respond emotionally if you know your financial condition and, more important, if you have faced the facts and prepared for the possibility of a severe economic chain reaction.

3. Set your goals and objectives.   You won't need a precise road map, but it would be a very good idea to have your goals clearly in mind. Naturally these goals will differ based on a multiplicity of variables, such as your age, profession, tax bracket and so on. Furthermore, the severity of the Y2K crisis will be an important factor. Your minimum goal should be protection of assets. Your maximum goal should be profit.

4. Avoid being influenced by those who offer simplistic solutions.   Every major turn in market events will usher in a cadre of Y2K financial "prophets" who will claim to have the ultimate answer to problems confronting the economy and society. Some may offer valid recommendations and alternatives, but it is more likely that their solutions will not be effective. There is no ultimate answer to the problem of protecting your assets; however, a well-planned and diversified portfolio is best. Although simplistic answers and explanations will be attractive and seemingly logical, simple solutions are not likely to work.

5. Believe in yourself!   When others claim to know what's right for you, don't follow their lead until you've had an opportunity to fully evaluate their claims, analyses and forecasts. Develop your own specific strategies and act on the basis of your own observations. Trust in your opinions, but don't trust blindly. If you take the time to learn about the history of the market patterns, economic cycles, crashes and panics, then your own work will serve you best. Keep an open mind, evaluate all reasonable inputs, make up your own mind and then take action.

Summary

If a Y2K crisis develops, then it will be important to be prepared both financially and psychologically. This chapter provided specific suggestions regarding emotional preparedness for the possible Y2K crisis or, for that matter, any economic or market crisis.

ARE YOU READY?

The study of economic history teaches that there will always be crises and euphorias.

> To define is to kill, to suggest is to create.
> —Stéphane Mallarmé

Stock market lows and economic lows will often develop concomitant with crisis, panic and pervasive pessimism. Stock market peaks and economic peaks will often develop concomitant with euphoria, optimism and rampant speculation. Some peaks and troughs will present major opportunities for the investor while others will prove to be only minor opportunities. The astute investor will learn how to recognize the signs and symptoms that precede market tops and bottoms. Within this context, the Millennium Crash is likely to be nothing more and nothing less than another crisis. As such, it will create market opportunities for the investor who is prepared.

The Y2K situation changes daily. Investment opportunities will present themselves as the situation unfolds. Markets will become more reactive to Y2K news and developments as the Year 2000 approaches. But whatever happens as a result of Y2K, there will be even more opportunities once 2000 has come and gone. Therefore, you are best advised to maintain a broad perspective.

What I have attempted to do in this book is to provide you not only with a concise explanation of the potential problems and its causes, but also with solutions and strategies. My advice has been as specific as possible given the differences in financial ability and investment goals from one individual to the next. In planning your specific strategy, always consider your financial goals within the framework I have provided.

I urge you to keep in touch with my latest thoughts, observations and analyses via my website: http://www.trade-futures.com. I can be reached via e-mail: jake@trade-futures.com should you have any questions, comments or observations. I will gladly send you a free copy of my latest market analyses either in stocks and/or commodities; just drop me an e-mail request at the above address.

REFERENCES
AND RECOMMENDATIONS
FOR FURTHER READING

Bates, David S., "The Crash of '87: Was It Expected: The Evidence from Options Markets." *Journal of Finance*, July 1991.

Bierman, Harold Jr., *The Great Myths of 1929 and the Lessons to be Learned.* Westport, CT: Greenwood Press, 1991.

Cutler, David M., Poterba, James M. and Summers, Lawrence H., "What Moves Stock Prices?" *Journal of Portfolio Management*, Spring 1989.

DeLong, J. Bradford and Shleifer, Andrei, "The Bubble of 1929: Evidence from Closed-End Funds." *Journal of Economic History*, September 1991.

Fisher, Irving, *The Stock Market Crash—and After.* New York: The Macmillan Company, 1930.

Galbraith, John Kenneth, *The Great Crash of 1929.* New York: Houghton Mifflin, 1972.

Greider, William, *Secrets of the Temple: How the Federal Reserve Runs the Country.* New York: Touchstone Books, 1989.

Kamphius, Robert W., Kormendi, Roger C. and Watson, J. W. Henry (eds.), *Black Monday and the Future of Financial Markets.* Homewood, IL: Dow-Jones Irwin, 1989.

Leland, Hayne and Mark Rubinstein, "Comments on the Market Crash: Six Months After." *Journal of Economic Perspectives,* Summer 1988.

Romer, Christina, "The Great Crash and the Onset of the Great Depression." *Quarterly Journal of Economics,* August 1990.

Shiller, Robert J., "Fashions, Fads and Bubbles in Financial Markets," in Coffee, Lowenstein, & Rose-Ackerman (eds.), *Knights, Raiders & Targets.* New York: Oxford U. Press, 1988.

———, *Market Volatility.* Princeton, NJ: MIT Press, 1991.

Schwert, G. William, "Stock Market Volatility." *Financial Analysts Journal,* May–June 1990.

Siegel, Jeremy, "Equity Risk Premia, Corporate Profit Forecasts, and Investor Sentiment around the Stock Crash of October 1987." *Journal of Business,* October 1992.

White, Eugene (ed.), *Crises and Panics: The Lessons of History.* Homewood, IL: Dow-Jones Irwin, 1990.

Wigmore, Barrie A., *The Crash and Its Aftermath: A History of Securities Markets In The United States, 1929-1933. Westport, CT: Greenwood Press, 1985.*

INDEX